High Whorling

A *spinner's guide*
to an old-world skill

Priscilla A. Gibson-Roberts

illustrated by the author

NOMAD

ISBN 0-9668289-0-9

**Library of Congress
Catalog Card Number 98-06818**

First Published in the USA by

NOMAD PRESS
PO Box 1082
Cedaredge, CO 81413

For the craft—past, present, and future

Contents

Acknowledgments

Quotations accompanying the spinner portraits beginning each chapter are taken from Soetsu Yanagi, The Unknown Craftsman, 1972.

To acknowledge all who have contributed to my work in high whorling would be overwhelming. So I will limit myself to those directly involved in the day-to-day reality of this book. First, my husband, Jack, for understanding my need to write this book and his willingness to become a partner in my work as well as my life. And, as always, my indispensable friends: Nelda Davis for always being there, no matter what; Noel Thurner for her enthusiasm and support in my every endeavor. Then my friends who made it all happen: Anna Zilboorg with her "we can do it attitude" and considerable talents as editor; David Oliver whose computer skills made putting it all together possible—without them, there would be no book. Lastly, Grace Crowfoot for *Methods of Handspinning in Egypt and the Sudan* and Bette Hochberg for *Handspindles*; they laid the foundation so many years ago.

Preface

I ambled down a long, circuitous route to find my niche in craft. It has taken more years than I care to recall. But the journey was rewarding—so many good memories as I sought what I refer to as "my destiny." I found it: high whorling is my calling. I will follow it wherever it takes me.

I began my involvement in spinning, as did many in the early revival days, with little guidance and make-shift tools, often of my own devising, all with few redeeming features beyond serving as a starting place. Accessibility to the few commercially available tools was limited for me, as I was primarily a nomadic knitter, moving through the boondocks of the arid West. What little advertising there was of tools and supplies appeared in weaving journals to which I had little access.

In retrospect, this was a minor inconvenience, as the commercially available tools were klunkers, little to no better than my efforts. I had no interest in an antique wheel, feeling that too much restoration was required for a functional piece of equipment, something that could be packed and carted hither and yon, wherever my geologist husband's work took us. I struggled along as best as I could with primitive, makeshift tools. In time, I came upon the spinning wheel of my dreams. It was a small, sturdy, handcrafted upright wheel, lovingly referred to as "Little Thumper," perfect for one with limited space and high mobility. I said goodbye to handspindles with little regret.

Thus began my odyssey of finding "self" within my dual craft of spinning and knitting. Textiles and ethnic clothing (both contemporary & historical) had long been my passion. I slipped naturally into the study of ethnic sweaters, recreating the old classics, always using my own handspun yarns. The result was my first book: *Knitting in the Old Way*. It was a survey—and depth was lacking. So I delved deeply into the sweater I found most intriguing: the Cowichan sweater, a garment made exclusively of handspun yarns, the early ones spindle-spun while today's are produced on the Indian-head adaptation of the spinning wheel. The result: *Salish Indian Sweaters* (an unfortunate title, using the tribal name rather than crediting the Cowichan band wherein the sweaters originated). By this time, I knew that it was not sweaters I wanted to document, even when they were made exclusively of hand-spun yarn. I wanted to find the roots of the craft, to get to the bottom of things. I needed to go back in time to find my soul.

Instead, I found soles: I studied historical socks. In the beginning, all were of European derivation, as they were accessible. But too few were of handspun yarns. I was not satisfied. Then a pair of Eastern socks came into my hands: exquisite handspun, handknit works of art. This was it—my soul truly soared, for here was the beginning, the roots of knitting. And it was dependent on spinning. Yes, many of today's are made of commercially spun yarns, but not the old ones!

In studying the socks I recorded in *Ethnic Socks & Stockings*, I discovered the use and value of the high whorl handspindle. It is a simple tool never replaced by spinning wheel technology through much of Scandinavia and the North Sea Islands as well as parts of Eastern Europe, the Middle East and Central Asia. In the northland, the spindle remained in use in conjunction with the spinning wheel. The spindle provided much needed mobility to allow spinning to continue regardless of one's location. In the eastern environs, it was and is the tool of choice., partly because nomadic ways survived in many areas, but even in settled communities the spinning wheel never gained popularity or was never introduced.

My first experience with high whorling was not just satisfactory; it was exhilarating! At last, a spindle I could relate to: no more fiddling and fumbling, just straight forward simple spinning. That first one was not a finely crafted spindle—just a plywood whorl, dowel and huge hook atop, but it was well-balanced and inexpensive.

With the acquisition of a finely crafted reproduction spindle from Iceland, I was off and running. There seemed to be little learning involved. Yes, I studied everything I could lay my hands on about the high whorl spindle and the various cultures that spawned them—mostly drawings and photographs, often in foreign language publications. Luckily, I seemed to know what to do to fill in the gaps. Instinct? Or written in my genes, as some say?

To me it seems even more than that. In part because I lived the life of a modern nomad so many years, moving from water project to water project all over the arid West, it felt much deeper. In ways that I cannot explain, I feel that in some far distant past, I traversed the Steppes of Central Asia, high whorling and knitting the hours away, as permitted by the demands of daily living—producing socks out of need, creating works of art out of desire. Not an easy life, stripped of all but necessities, facing the realities of a harsh environment, but a life lived close to the land, at one with the seasons and surroundings. Yes, high whorling seems more a matter of recall than learning. This feeling brings peace to my soul.

By now one might wonder what is so wonderful about high whorling. Simplicity first comes to mind. All my "necessaries" can fit in a small bag: my spindle, nostepinne

(Norwegian term commonly used today for a ball winding stick), niddy-noddy (skein winder) and occasionally what I refer to as plying rods (a set of old wooden knitting needles in my case), along with some prepared fibers

Then mobility. I spin anywhere, in small stretches of time whenever available, alone or in a crowd. This is something to consider for even those most devoted to spinning wheel technology—high whorling can significantly increase production in odd moments through the day, both at home and abroad.

Next, versatility is important. I can make any kind of yarn—woolen or worsted, high twist or low, fine or bulky—and always with precise control. I have read that some of the most meticulous weavers in Scandinavia would never dream of spinning their warp by any means other than a handspindle. To them, the spinning wheel was fine for the weft where minor inconsistencies were not a threat to a sound structure! And for those on a limited budget, high whorling is very economical. Homemade tools are an option for those with the necessary skills, while top-of-the-line handcrafted tools are readily available for a small investment. With the availability of high quality commercially prepared fibers, all one needs is a spindle, nostepinne, and niddy-noddy. Add to these a pair of hand carders and/or simple hand-held combs for those who want to begin with the raw fleece, as I prefer to do.

High whorling is fast, thus negating the most common complaint about handspindle spinning. A well-balanced high whorl spindle is a real production tool, regardless of the type of yarn desired. The spinner has the speed of an average spinning wheel plus minute control of the flow of fiber and twist that determines the ultimate quality of the yarn.

Last, but of utmost importance to me, is that high whorling is not taxing on the body. With mounting physical limitations, I look for those activities I can do in comfort. With high whorling, I can sit, stand, or move around. Since I am able to maintain proper body alignment, there is no strain on any part of my body. All this without suffering a loss of production!

Yes, high whorling is for me. No, I have not disposed of my two spinning wheels, but I must admit that I do think about it more and more frequently. Something that just sits idle, taking up space while acquiring layers of dust seems impractical when a simple, somewhat austere life is the goal toward which I strive.

I wish to stress that all of the following material is based on research applied to practical experience. Historical resources for the information I was seeking were scarce. My interests lay primarily in the non-literate cultures where much of our information is founded on assumptions. So when I could not find historical evidence of, for example, using the nostepinne for plying, I improvised a simple workable method, as would any true peasant. Thus the information imparted here is a way, which happens to be my way—it is not *the* way of high whorling. Each individual should take what is applicable and adapt it to suit their own working style. This is a hand craft—its rules are not carved in stone.

1

In Praise of The High Whorl

There are many types of handspindles, but most fall into one of two categories based on the position of the whorl on the shaft: the high whorl and the low whorl handspindles. On this topic I am very opinionated: the high whorl is superior. The low whorl spindle is the tool best known among western hand spinners because it has come down through our heritage from Colonial America and Western Europe. Not being part of our history and culture, the high whorl went unnoticed until recent years.

One of the reasons that use of the high whorl handspindle did not flourish in America and Europe was simple lack of information on its design and use. There had been little interest in the spinning techniques of the Middle East and Central Asia.

9

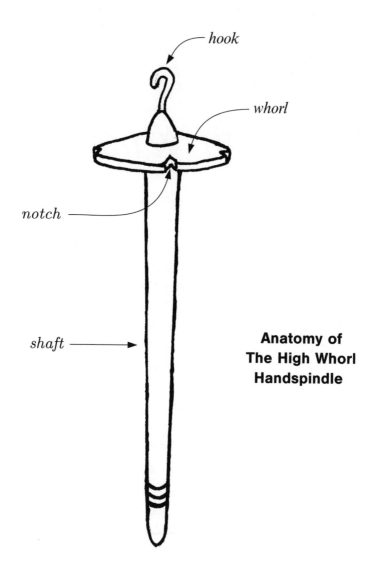

hook

whorl

notch

shaft

**Anatomy of
The High Whorl
Handspindle**

Only in archaeological studies of ancient tombs in Egypt do we find significant information about the high whorl handspindle. The friezes of various tombs clearly depict the use of this spindle spinning flax for the world-famous linens of ancient Egypt.

We can safely say that the high whorl handspindle has been in use for at least forty centuries (yes that's four thousand years and all but ignored by the 1960-70s spinning revivalists). (Grace Crowfoot, *Methods of Hand spinning in Egypt and the Sudan.*) Egyptians still call the whorl placed at the top of the shaft *ras el maghzal*: "the head of the spindle" (Bette Hochburg, *Spin, Span, Spun*). Though first used for linen, it is now more commonly used for wool.

The use of the high whorl handspindle was not limited to Egypt. It has been the tool of choice in diverse ethnic groups from the Bedouins and Sudanese northward to the Steppes of Central Asia and eastward to Eastern Europe. Nor was it limited to regions of the eastern world. It was common in Scandanavia and the North Sea islands. Although spinning wheel technology was embraced by many in this part of the world, it never completely replaced high whorling.

Advantages of the High Whorl

In recent years I have become aware of a groundswell of interest in the ease and efficiency of the high whorl spindle among both beginning and skilled hand spinners. So I offer here my prejudiced comparison of these two handspindles in common use.

Most obvious is the different position of the whorl on the shaft of each type of spindle. This position determines how each is rotated. With the high whorl, the lower section of the shaft is rolled on your thigh in one fluid motion, a technique that results in great speed with little effort. Twirling the upper end of the shaft with your fingers is required for rotation of the low whorl—a process I find much slower and more demanding on my hands.

Both styles require some means of securing the yarn to the top of the handspindle for spinning. A hook provides a quick means to secure the yarn on the **Classic High Whorl**. Many low whorls require wrapping under the whorl and around the lower shaft to secure the yarn before taking it to the top where it is attached with a half-hitch prior to spinning **(Low Whorl with Shaft Hitch)**. This is a fumbling procedure that must be done before and after spinning each length. Some low whorl spindles have a hooking device, but the spinner must still spiral the yarn, barberpole style, up to the top, to develop tension in the the yarn to secure it **(Low Whorl with Hook)**. After each length of yarn is spun, the process must be reversed to unwind the yarn before it can be wound on to the shaft for storage.

With the high whorl, the yarn is simply secured when it passes through the notch on the whorl, then up and around the hook for the spinning to continue—a straightforward process. Unhooking after each length of yarn is equally simple.

Classic High Whorl
Yarn passes through notch to hook

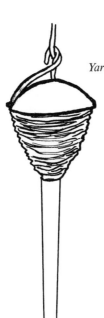

Low Whorl with Shaft Hitch
*Yarn wraps around lower shaft
and is half-hitched to upper shaft*

Low Whorl with Hook
*Yarn spirals up shaft, barberpole
style, and threads through hook*

2
Getting Started

This chapter is devoted to taking up the high whorl handspindle for the first time. It is for those who have never spun before as well as those coming to the high whorl with experience in low whorl or wheel spinning. Don't be concerned with the fine points of tools and techniques at this point. I'll get to them in the next chapters.

Get your hands on a good, basic high whorl handspindle in the 60-75 gram range and some carded wool roving (in a heather blend if possible—this will enable you to see the twist in the yarn more readily). I recommend one of the longer wools. I am especially fond of Romney for beginners. Six ounces will suffice to get you started. (See **Selected Suppliers** at the back of the book.)

You will familiarize yourself with the high whorl spindle by first using yarn rather than

Handwork, because it has nature behind it, has a way of fostering the good life.
—Soetsu Yanagi

15

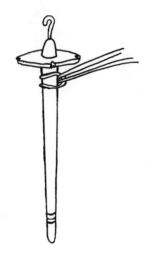

Securing the Yarn

Secure commercial 2-ply yarn to the shaft by drawing the ends through the fold

Threading the Yarn

Take commercial yarn up through notch and around the hook

roving. I suggest starting with 10-12 yards of two-ply wool commercial sportweight yarn. The first thing one must do is attach the yarn to the shaft. Fold the yarn in half, and secure it to the shaft by drawing the ends through the fold as in the figure **Securing the Yarn** and thread it through the notch and hook as indicated in **Threading the Yarn**. The spindle is now ready for use. You can now go through the steps of spinning without fear of dropping the handspindle.

I will go through the process step by step assuming you are right-handed. If you are left-handed, interchange the left and right hands in the following directions. (Spinning is an ambidextrous activity, but you have to start somewhere.) Stand for this part of the learning process as shown in the adjacent figures.

1. With the shaft in your right hand, throw the yarn ends across the left shoulder out of the way as illustrated in the figure **Beginning Twist**.

2. With your left hand, grasp the yarn about 24" from the hook.

3. Take the yarn up through a notch, then one clockwise turn around the hook.

4. You are now ready to experience the elegant way in which rotation is imparted to the spindle: by means of your thigh. With your right hand, roll the shaft UP your thigh as shown in the figure **Beginning Twist**. Then release the spindle, letting it hang suspended on the yarn, as illustrated in **Suspending the Spindle**. Twist will travel up the yarn to the left hand.

Beginning Twist
Begin to insert twist by rolling up thigh.

Suspending the Spindle
Allow twist to enter yarn with spindle suspended

5. Grasp the bottom of the shaft and unwind the yarn from the hook.

6. With shaft in hand, turn the whorl away from your body as shown in **Winding the Yarn**. Rotate the shaft clockwise to wind the yarn onto the spindle.

Go back to the second step and repeat the process again and again until you reach the end of the yarn. Wind the yarn off the spindle and repeat the process, except this time roll the shaft DOWN your thigh and wind onto the hook and onto the shaft in a counter-clockwise direction. Note that the former twist must be removed before twist can enter in the opposite direction.

Now add another step in the process. In step **4**, after the yarn is twisted, move your right hand up to hold the yarn while the left hand draws out another 24" of yarn. Release the twist from the right hand to allow it to continue to travel up to the left hand. This is the rough equivalent of what is called drafting with fibers. End by rolling UP your thigh on your last practice run with the commercial yarn.

Now you are ready to make your own yarn from the carded roving by making the twist hold the fibers together. I recommend sitting in this phase of the learning, process. Henceforth, you will continue to roll UP the thigh.

Leave some of the commercial yarn used for practice wound onto the shaft. You will want to have about 4" of the yarn extending above the hook. This yarn to which the fibers from the roving will be attached is called a leader. Tie the two ends of this doubled yarn together with an overhand knot. Pull off about 36" from the roving. Divide this section in four lengthwise strips. With one strip of the roving over your shoulder as the commercial yarn was before, draw out some fibers from the end. Lay this fringe of fibers through the loop formed by the knot of the leader and hold them against the roving in

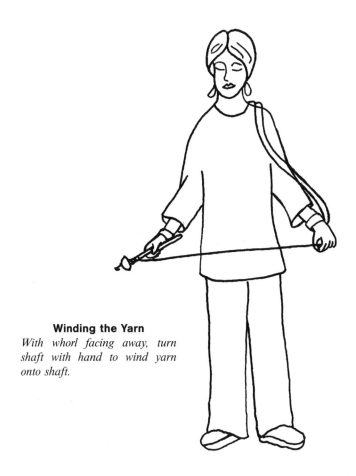

Winding the Yarn
With whorl facing away, turn shaft with hand to wind yarn onto shaft.

your left hand. Roll the shaft UP your thigh to insert twist into the fibers as in the figure **Drafting**. This time, support the spindle on your right thigh instead of suspending it. With the fibers attached you are ready to go through the spinning process, step by step.

1. Draw out fibers in small increments to elongate the roving to about 2-3".

2. Roll the shaft UP the thigh several times to build twist in this area as shown in the figure.

3. Let the handspindle lie on your thigh. Grasp the twisted fiber with the fingers of

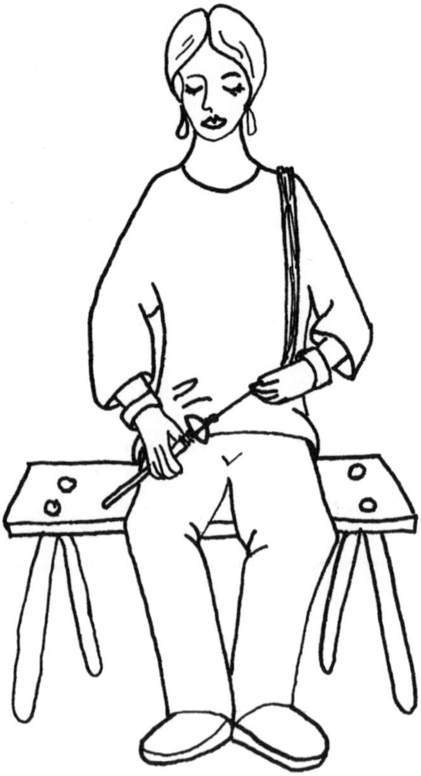

Drafting

Draft out short length. Roll several times to build up twist.

your right hand next to your left hand. Your right hand, through the pressure exerted by your fingers, now controls the twist.

4. Draw fibers out in the left hand about 2-3" as before.

5. Release the twist from the right hand as shown in the figure **Controlling the Twist**, freeing the twist to travel up the drafted fibers to the left hand. Repeat these steps until a comfortable length of yarn has been created. Wind it onto the shaft as before and start a new section of yarn.

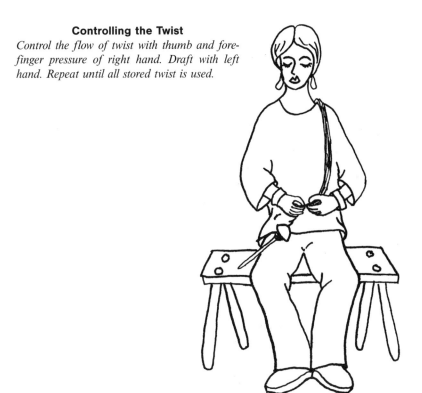

Controlling the Twist
Control the flow of twist with thumb and forefinger pressure of right hand. Draft with left hand. Repeat until all stored twist is used.

Once you are comfortable with this phase of learning, you are ready to put it all together in a continuous process. Still working while seated, draw out a short length of fibers. Roll the shaft with the right hand as before. Immediately after rolling, move your right hand up to control the flow of the twist while drawing the fibers out of the roving with your left hand. You should be able to draft more than once with each roll of the shaft. Work in this manner, **Winding On** at the required intervals, until you are comfortable with continuous drafting. Now stand up and work in the same manner with the spindle suspended.

When you come to the end of the roving strip, leave a small section unspun to overlap with a new strip. Should you break off while spinning, overlap the roving strip ends and continues the process.

You now have yarn. You have conquered the basics and are ready to go on to the fine points of selecting equipment and fibers as well as the technical aspects of hand spinning.

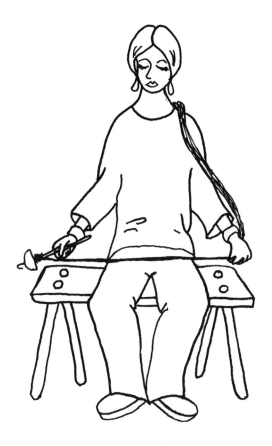

Winding On
Wind on as before.

3

Spindles and Supplementary Tools

Lovely things are almost always simply made.

—Soetsu Yanagi

The first consideration in choosing a handspindle is weight, for this determines what type of yarn you can spin comfortably on any given spindle. This does not mean that you must have a dozen or more spindles to spin a full range of yarn. For most spinners one is sufficient, as we tend to work within a fairly narrow range of yarn types. Two will cover a wide range of yarns, while a third should provide for a full range of yarns, from very fine to very bulky.

The size of yarn may be specified in several equivalent ways, such as its diameter. The most conventional specification is in wraps per inch (wpi). This is number of strands of yarn laid side by side which span one inch. (The diameter of the yarn, in inches, is the reciprocal of this number.) Yarn size in wraps per inch is directly determined (**Measuring Yarn Size)** by wrapping the yarn around a ruler, a small **Yarn Gauge**, or even a pencil, and counting the number of wraps contained within an inch.

The chart **Spindle Weights for the Production of a Given 2-ply Yarn Type**

Measuring Yarn Size

Wraps per inch (wpi) is the number of times a yarn wraps around an object to traverse one inch. A ruler, small yarn gauge, or even a pencil may be used. The yarn in the example is 7 wpi and its diameter 1/7".

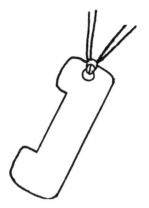

Yarn Gauge

Typical handcrafted wooden gauge on cord to hang around one's neck. Notch is one inch long. A cylindrical gauge (made simply by cutting a longitudinal notch in a dowel) is preferable to a flat, rectangular gauge because it supports a more even tension. Rotate gauge to draw yarn rather than winding on by hand.

Spindle Weights for the Production of a Given 2-ply Yarn Type

Spindle Weight	Yarn Type
10 gms	Lace (18+ wpi) to fingering weight (16 wpi)
25 gms	Shetland (15 wpi) to sports weight (14 wpi)
50 gms	Most versatile spindle weight, allowing production of all yarns except the very finest and the bulky—Shetland (15 wpi), sports (14 wpi), D.K. (13 wpi), knitting worsted (12 wpi), and bulky (11 wpi) weights
75 gms	Versatile for the heavier yarns, from D.K. (13 wpi) and knitting worsted (14 wpi) to the very bulky yarns (11 or less wpi)

may be used to determine the appropriate range of spindle weight for the desired final yarn size. This chart applies specifically to producing two-ply yarns, though it can serve as a guide for multi-plied and cabled yarns as well as for singles for the final product.

The Hook

All high whorl spindles are not created equal. There are a number of finely crafted ones available, and there are many that are poorly designed, but look quite elegant to the eye. Therefore it is important for you to learn the defining characteristics of a good high whorl spindle. To analyze the spindle we will begin at the top: the hook. Many will try to convince you that "a hook is a hook." Not so! A poor hook can make an otherwise good spindle all but unusable.

Why is the hook so important? You must guide the yarn onto and off the hook for every length spun. If this is not effortless, the spinning rhythm is broken and frustration rises.

I like a high, elongated hook, the highest point in the upper curvature centered over the base of the hook where it is attached to the spindle top. My favorite is a handcrafted brass "swan's neck" hook, followed closely by a commercially produced stainless steel hook from Scandinavia. The high peaked hook is another handcrafted style that can be good. It is bent rather than curved and is usually found on smaller handspindles.

On some spindles, the hook can appear to have little neck to it but on closer inspection,

Handspindle Hook Styles

Several hook styles found on handspindles. A vertical neck on the hook, as in a cup hook, is the least desirable.

Swan's Neck Hook

Elongated Hook

Peaked Hook

Shaft as Neck on Hook

Typical Round Hook with Vertical Neck (Cup Hook)

you can see that the shaft serves as the neck of the hook. In this case, the shaft should angle to the curvature at the top so that the yarn can slide up when wrapped onto the hook. If the neck rises vertically to a flat edge, the yarn may rest at the corner rather than the top of the hook, causing the spindle to wobble when turning.

Cup hooks are among the least desirable hooks for spindles, as the yarn is often secured on the neck rather than at the top of the curve. A more suitable commercially available hook is a fine gauge ceiling hook, a very sturdy hook somewhat similar to the swan's neck described above.

The Whorl

Next is the whorl itself. Its shape, size and weight vary considerably with the materials used. I cannot cover all the possible variations, but will suggest some general characteristics to consider in selecting your spindle. The first is the position of the whorl on the shaft. In most cases it is at the very top of the shaft, though some are located up to a quarter of the way down the shaft. Spindles with the whorl at the top tend to dance a bit when first starting to load with yarn. They settle down after several lengths of newly spun yarn have been wound on.

The down-shaft whorl is more stable from the first turn of the spindle; it also allows one to either turn it by hand or roll it on the leg for rotation. On filling, those with the whorl at the top can contain more yarn than spindles with a down-shaft whorl. Personal pref-

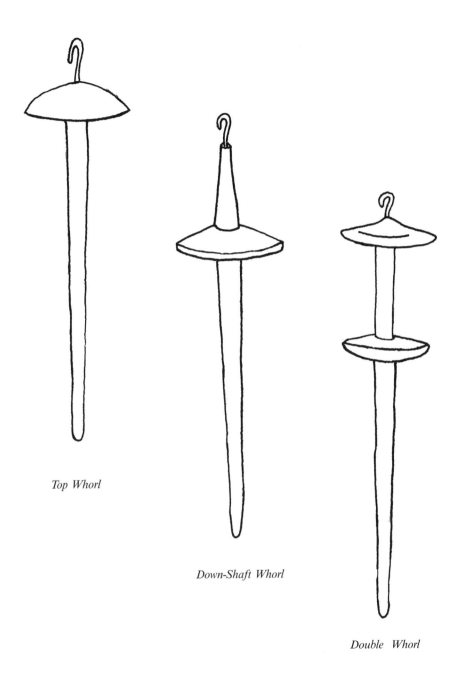

Top Whorl

Down-Shaft Whorl

Double Whorl

Three Types of High Whorl Handspindles

erence (what feels right) becomes the determining factor in selection.

Whorls can be permanently attached or removable. The attached are more bulky when stored, more prone to minor scrapes and bruises (though they can also develop a comforting handspindle patina) when carried around. The removable whorl style is easy to store, but once yarn is wound on the shaft, this advantage is lost since removing the whorl will distort the cop.

Removable whorls are either secured with a friction fit of whorl to shaft or by being screwed onto a threaded shaft. Friction fit whorls may be attached from the base up or the top down, both with attendant disadvantages. Unless carefully fitted to securely stay in place, a friction fit put on from the top can slip upward from the pressure of the yarn. Similarly, one put on from the bottom up can slide downward quickly if bumped at the base of the shaft. In my opinion, removable whorls are most desirable when a single shaft is designed for two whorls, one the primary whorl for spinning and a second, heavier whorl for plying.

Then there is the double whorl spindle with one at the top and a second spaced part way down the shaft. The lower whorl serves to weight the spindle in order to steady the rotation until the first few lengths of spun yarn are wound on. As the cop (spun yarn wound on the shaft for storage) builds, the lower whorl can be removed. This second whorl also provides extra pull for heavier yarns, greatly extending the range of yarn sizes possible. The second whorl also provides additional weight for plying.

The Notches on the Whorl

Notches on the whorl are imperative in my opinion—and many beautiful spindles do not have them because they would break the aesthetic design of the whorl. As my high whorl spindles are tools first, works of art second, I add notches if they are not provided.

Flat and Domed Whorl Notches are common. On a domed whorl, a notch can be cut at an angle through the edge where the dome intersects the flat base. On a flat whorl, the notches can be cut vertically through the side. They can be the classic "V" notch often found on old spindles, a straight edge vertical cut, or a semi-circle. I much prefer the semi-circle notch because it secures all yarn diameters without slippage. No tiny notches; you want one of sufficient size to both spin singles and to ply the yarn.

The **Placement of Notches in Relation to Hook Opening** is also important. If there is only one notch, it can be located directly in front of or behind the opening of the hook. A notch behind the opening of the hook is preferable to one in front as the yarn will not catch in the corner of the hook. With two notches, placement can be on each side of the hook (my preference) or one directly in front and one directly behind the hook. With three notches, the first should be directly in front or behind the hook opening with the other two evenly spaced around the circumference.

"V" notch in vertical edge.

Semi-circular notch on vertical edge.

Notch cut at angle on base of dome.

Flat and Domed Whorl Notches

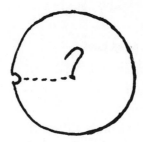

*One notch placed directly in front
of or behind hook opening*

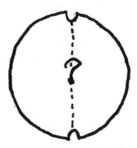

*Two notches placed on opposite sides of
hook and perpendicular to hook opening*

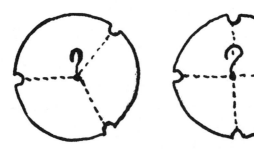

*Three and four notches equally spaced around
whorl with one directly in front of hook opening.*

Placement of Notches in Relation to Hook Opening

The Shaft

The shaft is the final portion of the spindle to consider. Although it may seem unimportant, the shaft can make spinning pleasure become pain. First, beware of the dowel as a shaft. Dowels have a tendency to warp in time. This kind of spindle can serve as a learning tool, but when warped, the spindle wobbles and becomes a frustration.

A shaft turned on a lathe is much more dependable over the long run. A disadvantage of the turned shaft is that most are so smoothly finished that the yarn will not pack densely around the shaft, tending to shift downward. Unless care is taken when winding on, you can end up with a mushy cop.

A shaft made with a draw knife will have flattened areas not visible to the eye, but readily felt by the hand. These slight irregularities allow the yarn to grip the shaft for ease in winding on. An additional advantage is that irregularities resist sliding when rolling the spindle on the thigh, so they develop greater speed of rotation. Grooves cut vertically on the shaft also serve these purposes.

I like a tapered shaft rather than a straight one. A tapered shaft allows the cop to slip easily from the shaft onto a plying rod. Turnings on the shaft prevent easy removal of the cop.

Finally, the shaft must be long enough to accommodate both the yarn and the hand. Small spindles require only the fingers for rotation, so they do not have to be as long as heavier spindles which, when spinning a

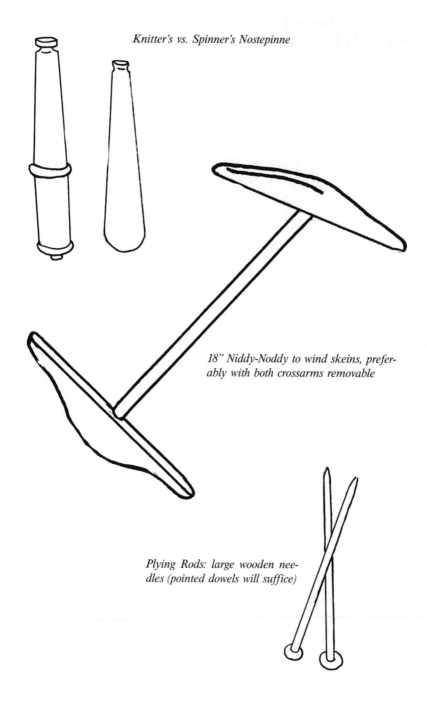

Knitter's vs. Spinner's Nostepinne

18" Niddy-Noddy to wind skeins, prefer-
ably with both crossarms removable

Plying Rods: large wooden needles (pointed dowels will suffice)

Supplementary Tools for High Whorling

heavy yarn, require the full force of the hand. In general, the shaft on the larger spindles should be between 12" and 15" while small spindles have a shaft between 7" and 8-1/2."

I must stress that the *perfect* spindle does not exist. For spinners learning their skill, I recommend a good quality basic tool in the 60-75 gram range. With experience, each individual can then select a spindle that possesses characteristics that person finds most desirable. Unless you are a collector, do not buy for looks alone—the high whorl spindle is a tool first for the real spinner. (See **Selected Suppliers** at back of book for sources of my favorite working spindles.)

Supplementary Tools

When you are serious about high whorling, you will want to consider adding a nostepinne (ball winding stick), a niddy-noddy (skein winder), and occasionally rods for multi-ply yarns. These are readily available, most are serviceable. I do recommend a nostepinne that has a steep angle from base to top with few decorative turnings and a shallow groove for securing the yarn (a deep groove can, on occasion, snag the singles when using the nostepinne for plying). I suggest something smaller than the old standard 2 yard niddy-noddy for ease in winding off of the spindle. I much prefer a 1-1/2 yard niddy-noddy because it is easy to use when seated without stretching one's arms into awkward positions. Removable crosspieces are a big plus, as they make the niddy-noddy much easier to carry around.

4

Fibers and Fiber Preparation

Fiber selection and preparation is the key to good spinning. I will limit my discussion of this subject for a number of reasons. First, I feel spinners new to high whorling should concentrate on their high whorling techniques, working with the high quality prepared fibers available today. The study of fibers is a field in and of itself with sufficient information in print for you to study as your skills and needs develop.

I will offer my approach to the topic, principally related to wool since that is the fiber of choice for most spinners. I will concentrate on simple hand held tools for fiber preparation only, for these are more appropriate to high whorling than studio equipment. I will cover the basic information for those who are not familiar with the various terms and techniques.

Work done with the heart and hand is ultimately worship of life itself.

—Soetsu Yanagi

Fiber Choice

All traditional fibers can be spun on a high whorl handspindle. For the short, fine, and/or slick fibers (cotton, cashmere, alpaca, kid mohair, angora, etc.), use the spindle supported on the thigh. With experience, many find that these fibers can also be spun suspended on the lightweight spindles, especially if blended with a small amount of wool. Wool and other longer fibers (flax, hemp, mohair, etc.) can be spun on a suspended spindle with ease.

Wool, the easiest fiber to spin, can readily be spun supported on the thigh for a light, lofty, low twist bulky singles for knitting sweaters or suspended for a high twist, dense, sock or warp yarn—and every yarn in between. As wool gives us the full range of possibilities, I will concentrate on its use with comments about some of the other fibers. Bear in mind that I am primarily a knitter and sometime tapestry weaver, so many of my comments are directed to these uses with which I am most competent.

Wool comes in several grades: fine, medium, long (coarse), and braid. Fine wools are shorter, highly crimped fibers such as Rambouillet, Merino and Cormo. These wools are great for garments worn next to the skin, ideally suited for fine lace to sport weight yarns. But with their crimp, which helps to absorb the twist forces, they can also be spun into knitting worsted weight yarns. These wools are more difficult to handle and should be avoided by the beginner, whether in the fleece or as prepared fibers.

Medium wools are longer than the fine wools, with a more open crimp; examples include Finn, Corriedale, and Columbia. These wools are easy to use and can be spun in a wide range of weights, from fine yarns to the bulky singles for knitting. Long wools, with their open wavy crimp, subtle sheen and coarser fiber lend themselves to dense, durable yarns for handweaving, socks, outer garments, warp yarns, and rug weft. Braid wools are very coarse, often hairy and thus used as a rug wool. While practicing your high whorling skills, I suggest working with the medium wools and the finer long wools (Romney is my preference), experimenting with the other wools when comfortable with the tools.

I spin mostly wool. Living at an elevation of 6300 feet on the pinion-juniper steppe of the arid Colorado Plateau makes wool ideal. Even though we have barefoot days during the summer, the air chills rapidly as the sun sets, making a light wool shawl and socks delightful—and my big, thick woolly Cowichan vests and sweaters make the bright, sunny but cold winters a pleasure.

For fancy socks, I might chose the medium wools for softer, but less durable socks—the kind that I use for dress wear (which means good blue jeans to me). Among the medium wools, I prefer Finn (caressingly soft with some sheen), Columbia (readily available in the West), and Corriedale (soft sheen and quite durable).

For everyday socks, I prefer the long wools, as they are more durable. But I usually choose those in the finer range of the grade. My favorites are a crimpy Romney or finer Lincoln, which give me sheen, durability, and the range of natural colors I crave.

Crossbred wools are another option. These wools come from a long-term breeding program designed to create wools with specific characteristics, not necessarily to develop a stabilized breed. I am particularly fond of Finn-Lincoln and Karashire, a trademarked Karakul-Shropshire cross. I sometimes think of these as my favorites, being the best of both worlds with characteristics of both medium and long wools, with a good natural color range.

I also use some dual-coated wools from the primitive breeds (short wooly undercoat with long silky outer coat for socks, while those with coarser outer coats are great for tapestry weaving). My natural favorite is the little churro brought into the Southwest by the early Spanish explorers—the lamb's wool is great for socks! This breed is often called Navajo churro for its historical use in Navajo blankets and rugs. Karakul lamb's wool can also be wonderful, while the adult fleece was traditionally used by village weavers in the Middle East and Central Asia. Spelsau from Norway is also lovely—the long wool provides durability in combination with the cushioning of the short woolly undercoat. Although those with sensitive skin might find it prickly in socks, it is unsurpassed for tapestry work.

To enhance the characteristics of a given fiber, I often blend with other fibers. A small proportion of kid mohair added to wool makes socks of incredible silkiness. Adult mohair with wool for the heel-toe sections will make them wear like iron— and when dyed, give a sparkle of more intense color, letting the world know that something special has been created. Angora and wool can be used for light socks that are incredibly warm. Yes, the angora has a tendency to felt on the inside, but this does not alter its value.

There are times that I do not want wool socks. I want cotton socks—but, as a knitter, I am somewhat disdainful of cotton's lack of elasticity. So what can I do to have the cool comfort of cotton with increased elasticity? I blend a small percentage of wool into the cotton (using one of the fine wools, such as Merino). Fine wools are not ideal for socks, but this can be overcome in spinning: spin the singles, two-ply the singles, cable the two-ply—more on this technique later. These are just a few comments about how I approach fiber choice. Experiment to find out what works for you.

Woolen Versus Worsted

As stated above, fiber preparation is the key to effortless, consistent spinning. In standard preparation there are two choices: carded for woolen yarn and combed for worsted yarn. The preparation, in combination with spinning techniques, controls many of the characteristics in the final yarn.

I must also emphasize that when preparing and/or conditioning fibers prior to spinning, the fiber supply must be consistent with the yarn to be spun. A fine yarn requires a skinny fiber supply whereas a bulky yarn requires a fat fiber supply. An overabundant or insubstantial fiber supply leads to frustration and, all too often, defeat.

Carding and combing processes make yarns with widely diverse characteristics. Carded fibers are used to create a woolen or worsted-type yarn, depending upon the spinning technique selected. In the carding process, the fibers are roughly aligned with all fiber lengths present.

True woolen yarns are highly regarded for their warmth and light weight. The fibers most desirable for this type of yarn are the short (4" or less), highly crimped fibers. When spun with low twist, the fibers tend to push apart, many of the fiber ends protruding on the surface to create a halo. This halo creates dead air space to further enhance the dead air space within the core of the yarn, a great insulating property. The halo overlaps in the spaces between the stitches to mute pattern whether textured or colored. And with all the short fibers present and lower levels of twist to contain the fibers, these fibers are free to migrate to the surface to form pills. Unlike synthetic fiber pills which become shaggy and unsightly, wool pills tend to form and break off. Woolen yarns are not as durable as worsted yarns.

Combed fibers are used to create worsted yarn, and with skill can be used in a sleek, woolen-type yarn. The combing process results in the parallel alignment of the fibers with all short fibers removed. The longer, less crimpy wools (4" or more) are considered most desirable for combing. The resulting yarn is usually spun at higher levels of twist to enhance density, durability and sheen. The fibers are twisted over their entire length, thus pilling is all but nonexistent. Pattern, whether textured or colored, will be clear and distinct as there is no halo to obscure the edges.

Worsted yarns are not as warm as woolen. As only the ends of the fibers protrude from a more highly twisted yarn, garments tend to be prickly to those with sensitive skin. In mill production, worsteds are flamed (gassed) to singe and remove the prickles. It is interesting that flaming is also possible for hand-crafted yarns.

In Armenia, socks knit from yarns of coarser wools were turned inside out, wet thoroughly, mounted on beautifully carved wood "blockers" shaped much like the sole of the sock, then passed over a flame to remove the prickles from the portion that touches the foot.

Woolen versus worsted—which do I prefer? Frankly I go through spells of combing and want only true worsted yarns. Then I will enter a hand carding phase. At some point, I decide, no, I want drum carded fibers. The preparation is fast and easy, allowing me to shade the yarn characteristics from soft woolen to dense worsted-type yarns.

Hand Carding

For carding, fibers are scoured. This is the term used for gentle soak cleaning with a mild detergent and plenty of hot water. The preferred cleansing agent is an agricultural animal shampoo called Orvus. Then they are air dried. The wool is then opened (teased) to remove foreign matter and loft the wool.

The final step is the actual carding. With two opposing faces of card cloth (special leather or vulcanized cloth embedded with many fine, bent steel teeth), the wool is passed from one carder to the other, repeating the process until all fibers are in rough alignment and homogenized. (See **Basic Principles of Hand Carding** on the following pages.)

This can be done on hand carders (which I use for all my fine fibers, including fine wool) or the drum carder (good for the medium and long wools). The carded fibers, when rolled into a tubular form (rolag) from the hand carders, are used to spin true woolen yarns. This will produce the lightest, loftiest yarn possible. The fibers from the drum carder are usually in the form of a large batt, although some spinners have a smaller version that produces a roving.

Drum carded fibers can be spun as a woolen yarn (somewhat more dense than yarn spun from the rolag) or as a worsted-type yarn for greater density and durability.

Peasant Combing

For combing, the wool is scoured in such a way as to retain lock structure, with some spinners scouring lock by lock while others carefully layer the fleece in the scour bath. The locks are lightly opened and mounted on hand-held combs, then passed from the stationary comb to the moving comb, the process reversed and repeated as many times as necessary. All short fibers and foreign matter will be retained on the comb for discard. The wool is then drawn off the comb into a long strand called a top. (See **Basic Principles of Peasant Combing** on the following pages.)

Storing Prepared Fibers

When the fibers have been prepared, they are stored until ready for use. There are several "packages" in which prepared fibers can safely be stored:

(1) **Rolags,** carded fibers in tubular form.

(2) **Batts**, flat sheets of carded fibers from hand or drum carders.

(3) **Roving**, batts condensed to form a long, fairly dense strip with just a hint of twist to maintain integrity, then rolled into balls.

(4) **Top**, combed fibers drawn out in a long strip which is stored like a roving.

(5) **Bird's Nest,** a circular wrapping of a hand combed top around one's hand, the end tucked in to secure it. (See **Creating a "Bird's Nest" from Top or Roving**).

Conditioning Fibers

After storage, the fibers must be conditioned prior to spinning. The rolag and the bird's nest need the least attention, at most a little shake to increase loft. More than rolags, I like a roving for my spindle work even when I have hand carded the batts. To make a roving, I fold the fibers in half across the face of the batt, then repeat the folding once

Basic Principles of Hand Carding

Use flat strokes for flat carders. Use wrist action to follow the surface of curved carders. (Flat back carders with offset handles are less stressful on hands for most.)

a. Hold carder, cloth side facing up. Lightly load by stroking teased fibers onto metal teeth.

b. Stroke top carder over bottom, beginning with lower third of fibers on bottom carder. Progress up adding 1/3 of bottom on each pass. Three passes are usually sufficient, although one or two extra are acceptable.

c. With card cloth facing up on both, transfer fibers from top to bottom carder. Place top carder 1/3 way down on bottom carder. Lightly press teeth together to catch fiber fringe. LIFT UP with with bottom carder. Resume carding as in (b) above.

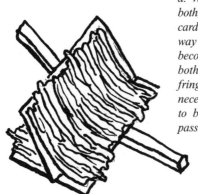

d. With card cloth facing up on both, transfer from bottom to top carder. Place bottom carder 1/3 way down on top carder (now become top carder). Lightly press both together to catch fiber fringe. Lift with carder below. If necessary, continue carding top to bottom—bottom to top, three passes on each.

e. To remove fibers from carders, lift from top then bottom, as in (c) and (d). With fibers released, use as batt, roll in rolag for woolen yarn, or fold and elongate for roving to spin worsted type yarn.

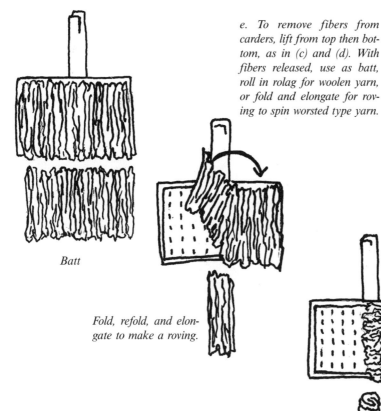

Batt

Fold, refold, and elongate to make a roving.

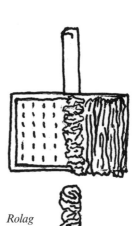

Rolag

Basic Principles of Peasant Combing

a. Load comb with clean, open locks until 1/3 to 1/2 of length of tines are filled. I like to lay down a thin layer. mounting cut ends, followed by a layer loaded at tip ends. Loading in this manner allows one to forget about a "directional" yarn. Be sure to catch only the ends of the locks allowing the fiber length to hang free.

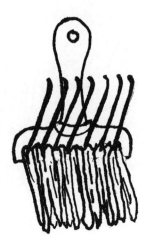

b. Stationary comb (left) should face away from comber. With moving comb (right) facing down, comb down through fibers at fringe, working upward into the fibers with each pass. Fibers will transfer to right moving comb. Clean short fibers and debris from stationary comb.

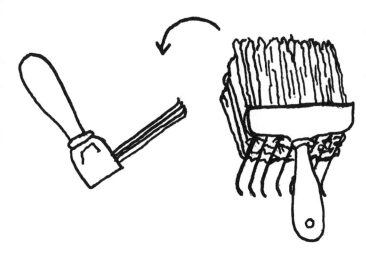

c. *Fibers are passed from roving comb to stationary comb, again beginning at fringe and working into mass of fiber with each pass. Fibers will transfer back to stationary comb. Clean moving comb. Repeat (b) and (c) until fibers are sufficiently prepared.*

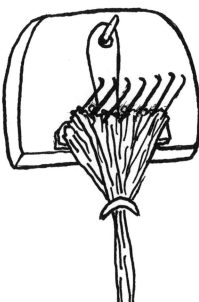

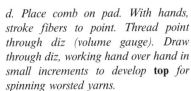

d. *Place comb on pad. With hands, stroke fibers to point. Thread point through diz (volume gauge). Draw through diz, working hand over hand in small increments to develop* **top** *for spinning worsted yarns.*

Creating a "Bird's Nest" from Top or Roving

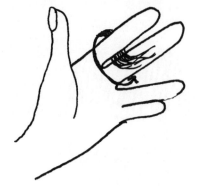

a. Tuck end between first two fingers. Wrap around 2 to 3 times.

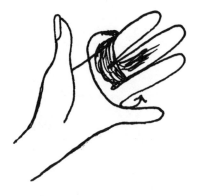

b. Add third finger and continue to wrap two to three times.

c Add fourth finger to complete wrapping. Tuck end to secure. Slip from hand and store. Pull from center when using.

more. I elongate this folded bundle just like the larger drum carded batts described below.

The thick batts off large drum carders need a good shake or two to loft them. Next, they must be divided into strips that can be elongated. (See **Converting Drum Carder Batt to Rovings.**) To divide a batt, I encircle each side of the batt with a hand, meeting in the middle to pinch and draw apart. I then repeat this process on the two halves to make quarters. The quarters, I elongate. With hands slightly apart (just a bit more than a fiber length), I grasp the strip in both hands, gently tug, using gentle jerking motions rather than a steady strong pull. I continue in this manner until the whole length has been elongated. As I move up the strip, I work to keep the strip even. I will grasp one hand at the end of the area just elongated while the other moves up. More than one pass at elongating may be required.

Commercial roving, whether carded or combed, needs special attention because the fibers are quite dense when compared to hand preparation. (See **Conditioning a Commercial Roving**.) I separate about a 36" length off of the roving (greater lengths are unwieldy to control when spinning). First, I grasp one end and shake it vigorously, then repeat the shaking at the other end. Just as with the batt, I then tear the roving into two equal parts, drawing them apart from the center, repeating the process on the halves for quarter sections. These strips are elongated the same way as the batts.

Converting Drum Carder Batt to Rovings

a. Divide batt from middle into two equal parts, Repeat with each half.

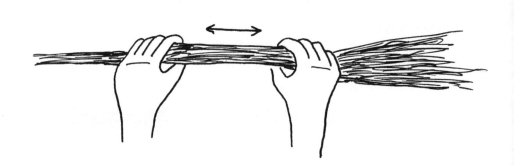

b. Starting at one end, gently elongate fibers between hands. Move slowly toward other end. Repeat if necessary. Use gentle tug and release motion to prevent tearing fibers apart.

Conditioning a Commercial Roving

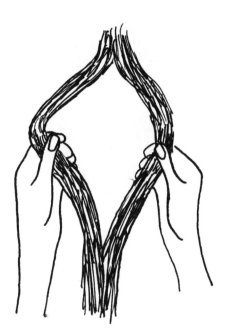

a. Separate about 36"– 45" strip from roving. At middle, divide into two parts. Redivide parts if necessary—how fine the parts should be depends on diameter of final yarn.

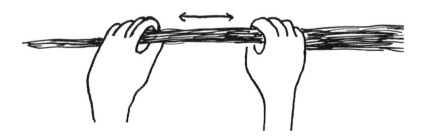

b. Starting at one end, elongate fibers with some snap in the tug and release motion in order to fluff and open compressed fibers.

Once conditioned, the fibers are ready to spin. Rolags need only be accessible to the spinner since they are small packages. But the other forms are now long strips which would interfere with the spinning unless somehow contained. In many areas of the world, the fibers would be put onto a long-handled holder (distaff) held under the arm or secured in a waistband.

I much prefer the Eastern nomadic tradition of **Coiling Roving on the Arm**. When spinning, one hand will control the spindle, inserting the twist, while the other hand will control the fiber supply. I use my right hand for the spindle, my left for the fibers.

First, I tuck the end of the strip under my Navajo storyteller bracelet (watchband, shirtsleeve, rubber band, whatever) to prevent the dangling end of the strip (when the roving will no longer coil around my arm) from catching into the developing yarn. Then I coil the strip around my arm counterclockwise, with the end coming out at my thumb.

I prefer this over a clockwise winding because I am most comfortable flicking my wrist clockwise to release a new section of fiber. Others prefer to wrap around the arm clockwise, the strip coming off the little finger side of the hand. This keeps the bulk of the fiber strip further from the twisting spindle, which is less likely to get accidentally caught into the developing yarn. Others randomly wrap, clockwise or counterclockwise, because it matters little to them.

Coiling Roving on the Arm

a. Tuck end under bracelet, watchband, or rubber band. Wrap around arm loosely counterclockwise for easy flick of wrist to release fiber supply.

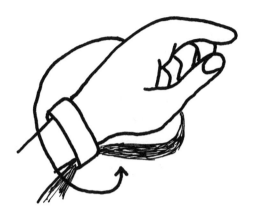

b. Tuck end under as a before, wrapping clockwise to keep fiber supply further from developing yarn.

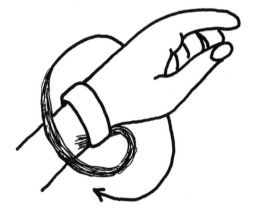

5

Spinning Technique

The principle of beauty of craft is no different from the law that rules the spirit underlying all things.

—Soetsu Yanagi

A high whorl spindle is incredibly versatile. You can spin either suspended or supported to produce a full range of woolen and worsted yarns. By suspended, I mean that the handspindle hangs from the newly created yarn while you continue to extend its length. Many refer to a spindle used in this manner as a drop spindle. I prefer the more descriptive "suspended" terminology to "drop" because of the unfortunate connotation that "drop" carries. You can either stand or sit when using the handspindle in this manner.

Supported means that the shaft rests on something, in this case on your thigh. This way the yarn does not have to support the weight of the handspindle. Used in this manner, spinning is done while seated. In some parts of the world a supported high whorl

"Z" Spun Yarn

A "Z" twist in the yarn results when the handspindle is turned clockwise. Most singles are spun in this manner.

"S" Spun Yarn

An "S" twist in the yarn results when the handspindle is turned counterclockwise. Yarns are usually plied in this manner. When balanced, the fibers in the "Z" twisted singles are aligned vertically in the ply.

spindle is referred to as a lap spindle. A supported spindle is ideal for soft woolen yarns and the big, bulky singles so hard to spin on a wheel, while a suspended spindle lends itself to spinning denser woolen and high twist worsted yarns. Used either way I prefer to spin while seated on my slanted seat weaver's bench or a stool.

Direction of Rotation

A handspindle rotates in two possible directions. The resulting yarn from the two directions is known as either "S" or "Z" yarn. Rolling the shaft of the handspindle clockwise results in a **"Z" Spun Yarn**. The angle of twist on the yarn will match the center portion of the letter Z. Conversely, rolling the shaft counterclockwise results in a **"S" Spun Yarn**. Again, the angle of twist will match the center portion of the letter "S." As a general rule, singles are spun "Z" and plied "S". This is true for knitting yarns, whereas the opposite is true for crochet. In crochet, the wrapping action of yarn around the hook removes the "S" twist. In time you might find yourself with two strands instead of a plied yarn. Also, some weavers like to use singles to play the "S" against the "Z" for textural effects.

And how do I determine what is clockwise and what is counterclockwise? By looking down onto the top of the whorl. If the top of the whorl is turning in **clockwise rotation**, you will have a "Z" yarn. If the top of the whorl is turning in **counterclockwise rotation**, you will have an "S" yarn.

When using the high whorl suspended, roll

the shaft up on the right side of the thigh for "Z", down the right side for "S". Or, roll down the left side of the thigh for "Z", up the left side for "S" (see the figure **Direction of Roll on Leg** on the following page). When standing, I roll the shaft on the outside of my leg. When spinning suspended while seated, I spread my legs to work on the inside of my left thigh as this allows me to maintain good spinal alignment.

Working on the outside of my right thigh requires twisting my spine to get my arms into position. If I am spinning supported, I use the outside of my right thigh, drawing the fibers to the left across my lap, in order to maintain spinal alignment.

When rolling up, begin the roll at the heel of the hand and when reaching the finger-tips, give a flip of the fingers to maximize the speed of rotation. When rolling down, begin the rotation with the tip of the fingers, pushing off with the heel of the hand for greater rotation.

You can use any combination of the up and down roll that is comfortable. This means that you can do all the rolling on the right side by coming up for "Z" and going down for "S". Or, all the rolling can be on the left side, down for "Z" and up for "S". You can also choose up on the right for "Z" and up on the left for "S", while a downward roll on the left is for "Z" and on the right for "S".

I have tried the various combinations and prefer to use the upward roll on right and left. This means that the hand controlling the spindle shifts from right to left. In other

CounterClockwise Rotation

Counterclockwise rotation viewed from the top of the handspindle results in an "S" twist.

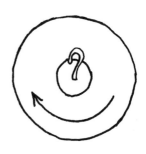

Clockwise Rotation

Clockwise rotation viewed from the top of the handspindle results in a "Z" twist.

Direction of Roll on Leg

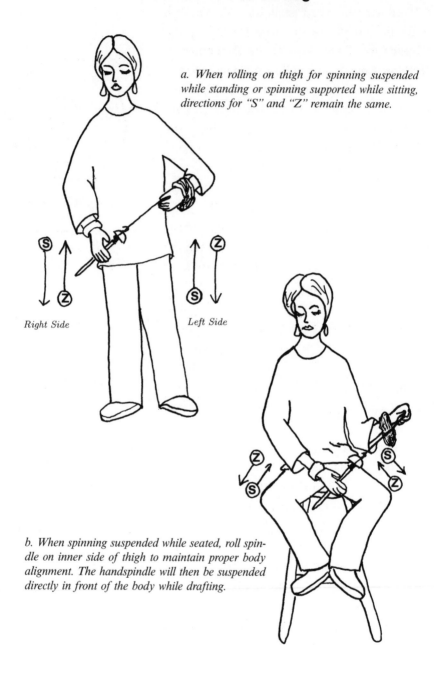

a. When rolling on thigh for spinning suspended while standing or spinning supported while sitting, directions for "S" and "Z" remain the same.

Right Side   Left Side

b. When spinning suspended while seated, roll spindle on inner side of thigh to maintain proper body alignment. The handspindle will then be suspended directly in front of the body while drafting.

words, I hold and control the handspindle with the right hand and the fibers with the left hand when spinning my singles "Z". When plying, I control the spindle with my left hand with the singles in my right hand. I have found this to be most comfortable because each arm performs similar activities. Working this way has another advantage. Most of the spinning is "Z" singles, so releasing the handspindle frees the right hand in a split second. This means that I can drop the handspindle quickly to stir the boiling pot, grab the wayward child, answer the telephone, etc. Freeing a hand from the fibers is more complicated. On the other hand, plying off the nostepinne, I have no problem freeing either hand when necessary.

Beginning the Yarn

There are two ways to begin your yarn, that is, to attach those first fibers to the handspindle. One requires the use of a leader, the other does not. To use a leader, break off about a 36" length of brightly colored, fairly fine, plied yarn. (The illustrations for beginning with leader are those of Chapter 2 with commercial yarn serving as leader.) Fold the yarn over at the middle and secure the ends together with an overhand knot. Lay this knot against the shaft and draw the free end of the loop through the knotted end. Add a half-hitch so that the leader will not slip. You're ready to spin.

Draw out the fibers at the end of the fiber supply, tuck a few through the loop, then turn the shaft to insert twist. When the fibers are securely joined with a short section of newly spun yarn, wind it onto the shaft. I use this technique when I plan to pull the yarn from the center of the cop. The brightly colored leader eliminates any confusion about what to pull out.

The second way to start begins with the fibers themselves (**Beginning Yarn without Leader**). Fan out the end of the fiber supply, the tip between first and second fingers, the roving end between thumb and the remaining two fingers of the hand that will control the fiber supply (the left, in my case). With the handspindle in the other hand (my right),

Beginning Yarn without Leader

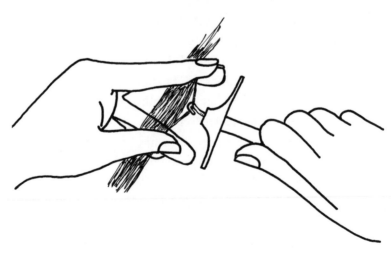

a. Fan fibers out in one hand. With hook, catch some fibers at side. Begin rotation to start yarn by turning spindle by hand.

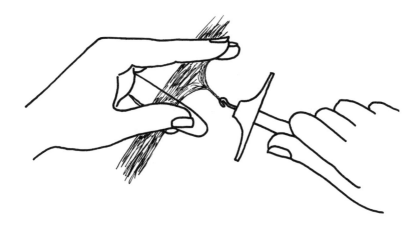

b. Develop short length of yarn turning spindle by hand.

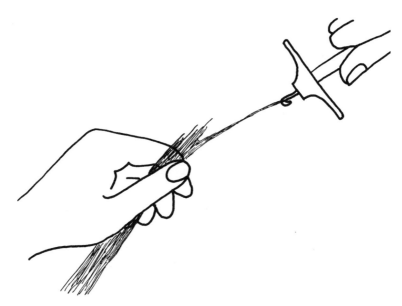

c. Swing developing yarn up to end of fibers. At this point, begin to roll shaft on leg while drafting out full length of yarn. Yarn is then removed from hook to wind <u>around</u> shaft, turing in same direction as the rotation.

catch some of the fibers onto the hook. At this point, the hook is at a 90 degree angle to the fibers. Rotate the shaft by turning it between your fingers in the proper direction, clockwise in most cases. As the twist begins to form the yarn, slowly shift the handspindle upward, toward the ends of the fiber supply, until the shaft is in a straight line with the fiber supply. When the yarn is a foot or so in length, rotate the shaft on your thigh until you have spun a yarn about a yard long. Slip this yarn off the hook and wind it around the shaft. By winding the yarn around the shaft, the yarn will be more securely held in place than it would be if you were to turn the shaft to wind on. The winding must be in the same direction as the twist. If you wind on in the opposite direction, the cop will become sloppy as the shaft fills with yarn.

The Spinning Process

When the yarn is attached to the shaft, the yarn passes through a notch to the hook. A turn of the shaft and the yarn is secured onto the hook. When spinning clockwise, you should wind onto the shaft clockwise and turn the shaft clockwise to secure the yarn onto the hook. This is necessary to maintain proper tension during spinning. The yarn is then spun to a comfortable length. To wind the yarn onto the shaft, grasp the base of the shaft and turn the whorl away from the body. A quick counterclockwise turn will release the yarn from the hook. With your hand still at the base of the shaft and the whorl away from your body, wind the yarn onto the shaft with a clockwise rotation. Now you are ready to take the yarn through the notch and onto the hook again. I like to leave 2"-3" of spun yarn above the hook. I then initiate my draft prior to rotating the shaft. This allows the twist to advance, giving me time to get my hands in position for drafting before the twist can build up in the already spun portion of the yarn above the hook.

I referred to "one turn" of the shaft as the means of **Securing Yarn to the Hook**. In actuality, one complete turn is only true when the notch is directly in front of the hook, whether spinning "Z" or "S". One-half turn is required if the notch is directly behind the hook opening, again for both "Z" and "S". When spinning "Z", if the notch is to the right of the hook opening, it will require a three-quarters turn, while a notch to the left of the hook will need about one and one-quarter turn. The opposite is true when spinning "S". When notches are on each side of the hook, some spinners simply catch the yarn under the hook (**Catching Yarn Under Hook**). I prefer the older, traditional wrap on the hook so that the yarn cannot come off if the handspindle is bumped or the yarn tension released.

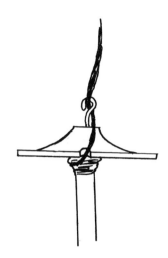

Securing Yarn to the Hook

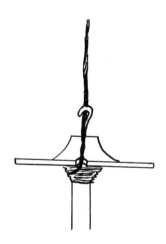

Catching Yarn under Hook

Here is **The Spinning Process**, step by step, for a "Z" spun yarn:

1. Begin by spinning the first section of yarn, either with or without a leader, rotating the shaft clockwise by hand.

2. Wind onto the shaft clockwise.

3. Take the yarn through the notch then onto the hook with a clockwise turn, leaving 2-3" of spun yarn above the hook.

4. Pre-draft a small section to initially absorb twist.

5. Roll the shaft on your thigh, quickly moving right hand into position to control the flow of twist.

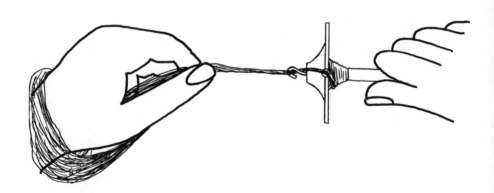

The Spinning Process: Beginning Twist

Leave small section of spun yarn above hook. Pre-draft fibers, allowing twist to travel into drafted fibers. Roll shaft on thigh. Upon release of shaft, move right hand into position to control advancing twist, releasing left hand to draft fibers.

6. Draft yarn.

7. Turning whorl away from your body, remove the yarn from the hook with a counterclockwise turn.

8. Wind the yarn onto the shaft clockwise. Repeat steps 3 through 8 to produce a full cop of yarn.

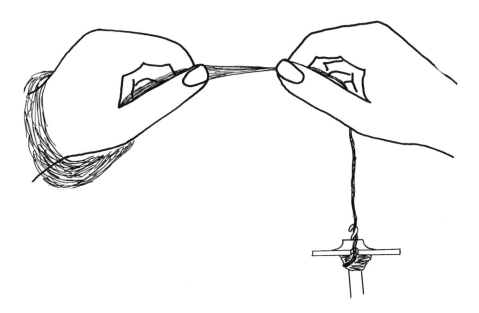

The Spinning Process: Drafting Zone Between Hands
Right hand controls flow of twist as left hand controls flow of fibers. Spun yarn passes over cupped fingers down to suspended spindle.

One additional concern for all spinners is proper **Alignment of the Hands**. You should avoid working with your wrists bent. Even slightly bent can lead to trouble in time, causing fatigue and possible wrist damage. When spinning, both the drafting hand and the hand controlling the flow of twist should be in a neutral position. This means that the "V" of the thumb and forefinger should be in a straight line with the middle of the arm, the fingers slightly crooked.

Building the Cop

Generally speaking, There are two ways to build a cop: (1) the beehive shape typical of Eastern spinning or (2) the spiraling cone typical of western spinning. A third, or hybrid, combining both is possible if that suits your working style. (**Three Styles of Cop**.)

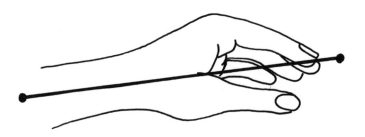

Alignment of the Hands

Alignment of the hand at rest. Maintaining this alignment, with a straight line through mid-arm to crotch of thumb and fingers, will reduce fatigue while preventing damage from repetitive motion.

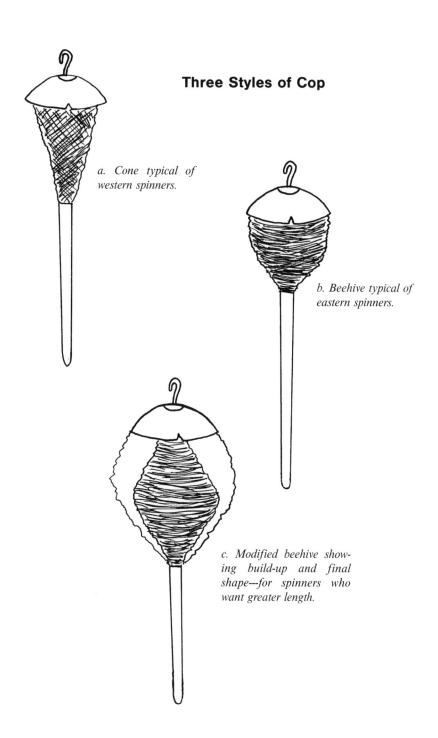

Three Styles of Cop

a. Cone typical of western spinners.

b. Beehive typical of eastern spinners.

c. Modified beehive show-ing build-up and final shape---for spinners who want greater length.

A beehive looks just like an inverted bee-hive in shape. The yarn is wound at the base of the whorl, then down the shaft, laying yarn by yarn, until the previous spun yarn has been covered. Then make a couple of turns to wind yarn onto the exposed shaft. Reverse and wind upward to whorl. With this method, the beehive is built from the top downward.

Occasionally, I will spiral upward (or down if you prefer) rather than winding side by side as this helps prevent the bottom from becoming loose. If you find the bottom has become loose, on the next winding down, when you reach the base of the cop, wind the yarn around the shaft rather then turning the shaft to wind the yarn onto the shaft, then spiral upward. Winding around the shaft is always tighter than turning the shaft to wind on.

Another technique to tighten the lower portion is crisscrossing the soft area, spi-ralling up then down several times. With practice, softening of the lower portion is seldom a problem. I prefer the beehive method as I find I can wind more yarn onto the handspindle without affecting balance, also it allows me to ply from the center of the cop.

An interesting variation of the beehive, for those who like to load the spindle heavily, requires building an oval shape slightly below the whorl (rather than at the base). The yarn is wound on, up and down the shaft, until the base of the whorl is reached. At this point, the winding continues to extend the point of the cop while filling in at the base of the whorl. Working in the manner makes for a heavy load.

A more elongated cone-shaped cop, which is typical of western spinning is made by spiraling the yarn down around the shaft the anticipated length of the cone, then spiraling back up. The next pass spirals down stopping one yarn wrap before the first, then turns to spiral upward. The cone builds from the bottom upward—just the opposite of the beehive. Proponents of this method say there is less danger of tangles, especially when removing the yarn from the shaft.

Vertical vs Horizontal Draw

Although the terms draw and draft are often used interchangeably by spinners, for clarity at this point I will use draw to describe the manner in which you use your arms. Drafting will define how the fibers are elongated between your hands. (See the illustrations of the **Three Types of Drafting** on the following pages.)

When spinning with the handspindle suspended, most people advocate a vertical draw, the Western method. In this case, the fiber supply hand is above the spindle hand. The hand freed from the spindle controls the flow of twist from spindle upward toward the fibers.

I find this method physically tiring to my arms and neck. My arms are continually extended higher and higher above my head, so I cock my head back farther and farther to see the yarn. This is especially a problem

Three Types of Drafting

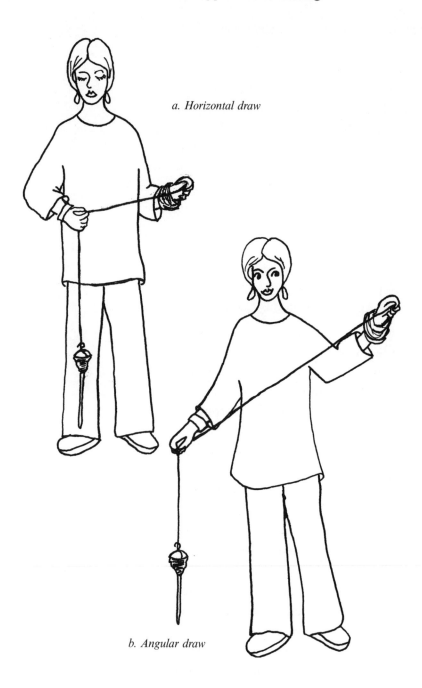

a. Horizontal draw

b. Angular draw

for those who have reached the age of eye-glasses with multi-focal lenses.

I much prefer the horizontal draw which I discovered in studying photographs of Eastern spinners. My arms remain in a relaxed position, half way between elbow and shoulder which reduces the physical stress on both arms and back. The drawing remains at one comfortable focal level, eliminating the chin up position of the vertical draw. The spindle is suspended from the hand controlling the flow of twist. The newly spun yarn passes across the crook of the fingers, hanging off the little finger in my case. Working in this manner provides extra insurance against breaking off and dropping the spindle.

When spinning supported, my draw is at a slight angle above horizontal, so my hand controlling the fiber supply is in about the same position as when spinning suspended.

Between these extremes is an angular draw, a blending of the horizontal and vertical methods. Some prefer working at an angle when they want to extend the length of the spun yarn before winding on, as you can comfortably extend the span between your hands.

c. Vertical draw

Woolen and Worsted Draft

The manner in which you draft the fiber determines whether you are spinning woolen or worsted. The main difference in drafting technique involves the control of twist. Drafting the fibers and advancing the twist are simultaneous actions when spinning woolen (called the long draw). They are separate actions, all drafting completed before twist advances, when spinning worsted (called a short draw). A supported handspindle is suited to the woolen style, especially those with low twist destined for knitting as singles. Suspended spinning lends itself to a worsted yarn or a somewhat denser woolen yarn. Neither woolen nor worsted is superior –they are just different.

Although carded fibers are usually spun woolen and combed fibers are usually spun worsted, your decision on the drafting technique should be based on the fibers you are using, how the fibers have been prepared, and the characteristics that you wish to attain in the final yarn. Carded fibers can be spun worsted for a more dense and durable yarn. Conversely, combed fibers can be spun woolen for a smoother, more lofty yarn.

There are two ways to spin woolen, both classified as the **Woolen Draw** or long draw: (1) spinning the diameter of yarn desired while drafting against the advancing twist and (2) quickly elongating a long, loosely twisted roving which is then attenuated to the diameter desired while allowing the twist to advance. In both methods, the fibers are drawn away from the handspindle. Either technique can be used, although staying ahead of the twist is considered the easier method when working suspended while either can be used supported. The newly spun yarn passes through the stationary hand which controls the twist, the yarn resting on the fingers to support the weight of the spindle. This auxiliary support, possible in horizontal drafting, allows for woolen spinning while working suspended. The loftiest of woolen yarns are spun from a rolag (often referred to as true woolen spinning), but I prefer to work with the longer lengths possible from using a carded roving.

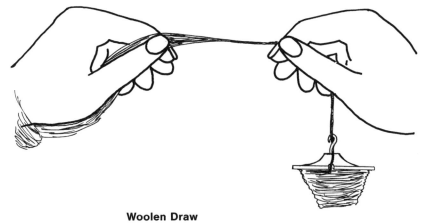

Woolen Draw

The woolen draw is defined by advancing twist at point of the drafting zone.

There is considerable argument about what is the **Worsted Draw.** And there is no definitive answer, since it depends upon which "expert" you are emulating, whether contemporary or historical. All agree that this is a short draw technique with the twist held back, not allowed to enter the drafting zone until all drafting is complete. To ensure that a smooth surface develops, the fingers controlling the flow of twist slide along the newly spun yarn as the twist enters. Then the picture gets cloudy.

One school of thought insists that you must draw the fibers out of the fiber supply with the right hand (toward the spindle), then slide back (toward the fiber supply) to slick down fiber ends while the twist enters behind the fingers. In this case, the stationary left hand is holding the fiber supply while the right hand moves to and fro. But if you let any twist enter the drafting zone, you may develop a slub at the point where the finished yarn meets the drafting zone. Should this happen, remember that a backward roll between thumb and finger can release enough twist to eliminate the problem. Smooth, steady drafting is necessary to avoid swinging the suspended spindle, though sway is not a great concern unless it becomes extreme.

The other school of thought proclaims that you must draw the fibers away from the spindle (with the left hand), allowing the twist to enter while advancing the yarn toward the spindle, smoothing the fibers as before. But, with this method, you can thin out the yarn if the drafting zone is extended too far—for which there is no quick remedy. You must break off and rejoin the fiber supply.

So which school of thought is *right*? In my opinion, it is a personal choice. I can work either way with the same results—any difference is not discernible. And I have seen those who make a hybrid of the two produce a wonderful worsted yarn. Again, it is not a matter of right and wrong, but one of what works for you. My preference? I usually pre-

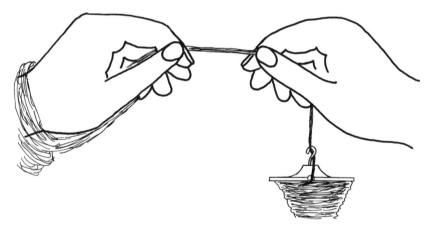

Worsted Draw
Worsted draw defined by absence of twist in the drafting zone.

fer to draw the fibers out with the hand controlling the twist. In either case, the idea is to draft about half the length of the fiber while keeping the twist out of the drafting zone. Then slick the fibers down between your fingers as you allow the twist to enter the drafted fibers.

An additional alternative for worsted spinning is a **Worsted Draw from the Fold**. A section of the top is removed (about the length of the longest fibers), folded over the forefinger and spun with a worsted technique, working from the fold. This is an easy method for spinning worsted, but the yarn will be highly "directional"—as the fiber ends are all lying in one direction, the ends will all protrude in one direction. Great for embroidery yarns! This method offers good control, but does not allow for the long fiber supply that I like.

Twist and Diameter

Controlling twist and diameter is often a topic of conversation among handspinners, especially those who use a spinning wheel. In some cases, the spinner carefully counts the number of treadles required for one complete revolution of the wheel, measuring the length of the draw to maintain a consistent yarn. This kind of gauging is not appropriate in high whorling. The principle involved can be stated in one sentence: Diameter is determined by the number of fibers allowed to remain in the drafting zone; twist is determined by the number of rotations allowed to hold the fibers together.

Diameter, as described in Chapter 2, can be measured by the number of times a yarn will wrap around a ruler, referred to as "wraps per inch" (wpi). Twist is specified in twists per inch, but this is difficult to measure. Instead, most spinners rely on a visual means to judge the amount of twist called "angle of twist." The less twist, the steeper the angle of twist.

Consistency of twist and diameter is another matter. Spinning yard after yard, skein after skein, takes practice. Many spinners judge their consistency by allowing a section to ply back on itself, making it possible to

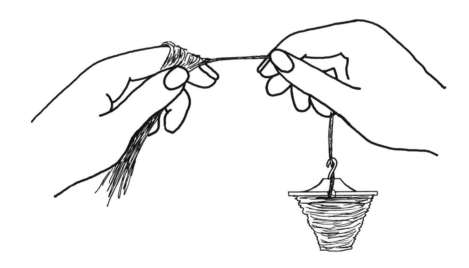

Worsted Draw from the Fold
Worsted draw spun from the fold. Some spinners prefer to fold over the fingers while others hold folded fibers between thumb and forefinger.

judge both diameter and angle of twist more readily. But if you simply relax the yarn to let it ply back on itself, you will not have a representative sample. The ply back inserts itself where the twist forces are the greatest—the thinnest portion of the yarn. In the proper **Preparation a Yarn Sample** you should spin about 20-24" of yarn tensioned by the weight of the spindle. With your free hand, fold this section in the middle. Holding the two ends together with the other hand, release the tension while running your fingers toward the fold. This will give you are representative sample of that section. You may then examine it using a Twist Gauge illustrated on page 84.

Since I cannot trust my memory, I make a **Sample Card** of the desired yarn by which to judge my consistency. I use about a 4"x6" piece of mat board, readily available in the waste basket at framing shops. I cut a short slit near the upper left corner of the longer side, repeating the slit in the lower right corner. I make a rolled knot at the end of the singles, then insert the yarn into the upper slit and wrap the yarn around and around the card to the lower slit. From this slit, I will take a 20-24" section and ply it back on itself as previously described. My sample card is now suitable for reference as I spin.

I use colored mat board for white yarn, white mat board for colored yarn. The sample must be made of newly spun yarn because the twist forces will be altered if the yarn is allowed to rest while wound onto the shaft under tension. For reference, just in

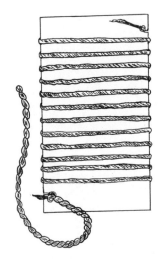

Sample Card
A simple visual guide for maintaining consistency.

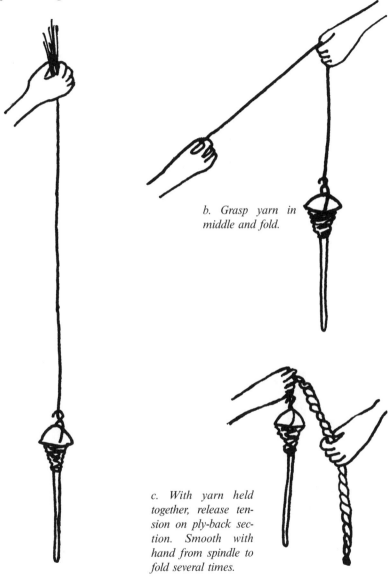

a. Newly spun length of 20-24" singles.

b. Grasp yarn in middle and fold.

c. With yarn held together, release tension on ply-back section. Smooth with hand from spindle to fold several times.

Preparation of a Yarn Sample

case I lay my work aside and forget what techniques were involved, I note the fiber, preparation, and spinning technique used.

An important point to consider: yarn can change in the finishing process. A woolen yarn can be altered dramatically, becoming shorter and more lofty. A worsted yarn does not change as dramatically. To be sure you will get the desired yarn, spin a small sample skein and carry it through the finishing process described in the next chapter.

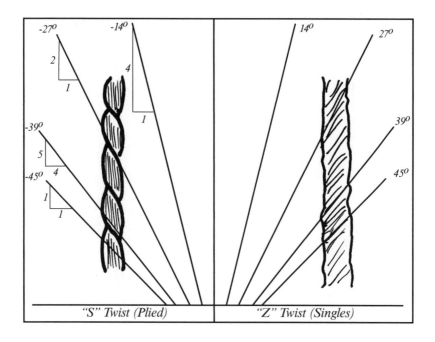

Twist Gauge

A twist gauge consists of angular rays of both positive (for "Z" twists) and negative (for "S" twists) angle. (Gauges may be commercially obtained or made with a protractor.) Twist angles for popular weights of yarn correspond to slopes of 1/1, 5/4, 2/1, and 4/1. Twist may be examined for consistency by laying yarn over gauge and aligning twist angle to angle of gauge. In the above illustration, the singles yarn is spun at 39° and the plied yarn at 27°.

Joining

Sooner or later your fiber supply will come to an end. You must now attach a new fiber supply to continue spinning. There is no big mystery to **Joining**, just common sense. If you spin all the fibers in the depleting fiber supply, you must lay the new fiber supply over twisted yarn with the new fiber supply to continue spinning. This leads to a weak join that can actually slip off of the newly spun yarn. Instead, stop spinning when there is a small portion of the depleting fiber supply left unspun. Fan out the fibers in this tail and those in the new fiber supply. Lay one over the other, and draft the two as a single unit.

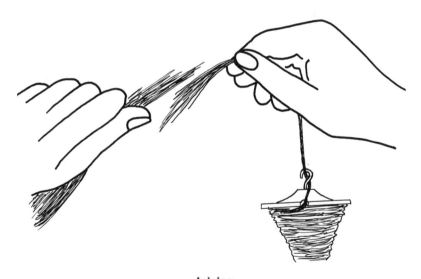

Joining

To make a join between old and new fiber supply, taper fibers on both ends, overlap to draft together while inserting twist.

Salish Indian Spindle

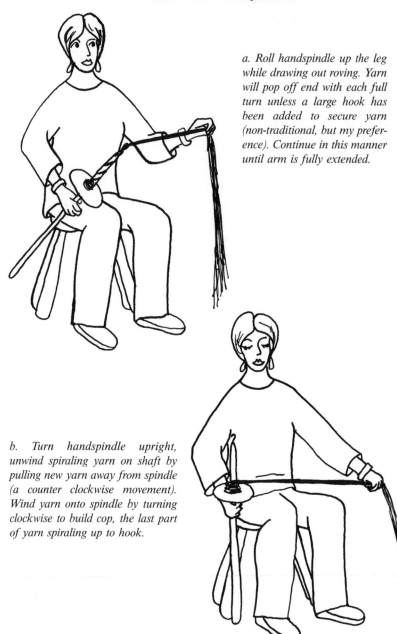

a. Roll handspindle up the leg while drawing out roving. Yarn will pop off end with each full turn unless a large hook has been added to secure yarn (non-traditional, but my preference). Continue in this manner until arm is fully extended.

b. Turn handspindle upright, unwind spiraling yarn on shaft by pulling new yarn away from spindle (a counter clockwise movement). Wind yarn onto spindle by turning clockwise to build cop, the last part of yarn spiraling up to hook.

This will make a smooth, sturdy join since the fibers from both ends are integrated into one unit.

What if you break off while spinning? This usually occurs when the fibers have thinned out. Too much twist rushes to the thin spot and breaks the fibers. The broken tail will have a lot of twist. I recommend breaking off above the highly twisted section in the yarn attached to the spindle, and removing any spun portion on the fiber supply end. With a backward roll between the fingers, remove twist from the yarn and fan out the fibers as much as possible. Then proceed with over-lapping and spinning as before.

Not Quite a High Whorl

I was slow to realize that my big **Salish Indian Spindle** is a type of high whorl hand-spindle. These spindles were used to spin bulky two-ply weaving yarns for blankets. After the introduction of knitting by early Europeans in the Pacific Northwest, the pri-mary use of the spindles shifted to creating the soft, bulky singles used for knitting their big, bold sweaters of natural colored wools.

As before, you must attach fiber to spin-dle. The method I learned begins with thigh spinning. The yarn is begun by rolling the fibers on the left thigh, drafting up and away with the right hand while rolling downward with the left. Wind the accumulating yarn in a figure eight around thumb and forefinger. When sufficient yarn has been prepared, fold one side over the other. Draw the yarn out of the the fold and wind it around the shaft clockwise as tightly as possible. Spiral the last portion up to the top and commence spinning, rolling the spindle up on the right thigh. The spindle should rest on the thigh at about a 45 degree angle when spinning.

I have departed from tradition by adding a large hook to my spindle. Now I can begin my yarn as with my other high whorls, attaching the fibers directly to the hook when spinning the initial section. When I spin, I do not need to worry about the angle of the spindle since the twist will go directly into the yarn (that is, it does not pop off the point). Working with a hook, drafting ahead of the advancing twist works as well as attenuating.

And for the finest spinning, I prefer to use the little **Akha Handspindle** from Southeast Asia, sometimes weighing as little as 8 ounces. Designed as a hand supported spindle for cotton fibers, I find it as delightful to use as a high whorl spindle. Traditionally, the shaft is turned by a flick of the thumb on the forefinger with the hand cupped to allow the twirling to continue in the remaining three fingers. In this case, drafting and inserting twist are two separate steps.

But I use the **Akha as a Classic High Whorl Spindle**, rotating the shaft on my leg. The only difference is in winding on: since the cop develops above the whorl, the yarn must spiral up the shaft to the carved hook.

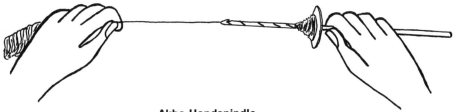

Akha Handspindle

In traditional use, the Akha spindle is twirled within the curl of the fingers. Spinning is in two steps: (1) twist to insert twist; (2) draft to extend yarn.

Akha as a Classic High Whorl Spindle

The Akha spindle can also be used as a high whorl spindle, the only difference is the need to spiral the yarn up the shaft. Incredibly fine yarns can be spun on this little spindle.

6
Singles, Plies, Cables

Turning loose fibers into a single strand of yarn produces singles yarn (sometimes mistakenly called a one-ply yarn). Singles can be spun together, that is, two or more strands united to make a plied yarn. And plied yarns can be combined again, this time to make a cabled yarn. Each combination requires the reversal of the spin direction. If singles are spun clockwise, they are then plied counterclockwise. When cabled, the clockwise spin is repeated.

Twist creates both force and energy. The pull exerted by a twisted fiber is the twist force. Rotation of the twist force around the strand of emerging yarn creates twist energy. Twist energy is stored semi-elastically in the stretched fibers. The twist energy stored in the yarn comes from the spin energy imparted to the handspindle by rolling it on your thigh. The reason the spindle spins down is that its energy is removed and transferred to the twist energy of the yarn.

A singles yarn is unstable, tending to twist back on itself, because once the fingers used to impart it have been removed, the twist force is unbalanced. If singles are plied in the same direction in which they were spun, additional twist force is applied to the yarn in the same direction as that applied to the singles, resulting in an even more unruly, harsh yarn. (**Examples of Twist Force in Plied Yarns**.)

By reversing the direction of twist in the ply from that of the singles, the twist force from one single is put opposite to that of the other and the plied yarn has no unbalanced twist force. (Think of the singles applying the force to one another that the spinner's fingers formerly applied).

The plied yarn still contains a net twist energy locked in the individual singles, but the net twist force of the ply has been reduced to zero. A balanced yarn is a yarn with no net twist force (though with twist energy). Yarn free of net twist forces is said to be relaxed.

Cabling is the process of plying together yarns which are already plies. If the plies to make a cable are balanced, it is obvious the cable will be unbalanced since new twist force is imparted to the plies rather than allowing their individually unbalanced forces to come into balance. To make a balanced cable, one must begin with *unbalanced* plies— plies that are *over-plied*. When these plies are cabled (again in the opposite direction from that in which the plies were created), the cable will be balanced.

Balanced plying or cabling is a way of neutralizing the twist force without neutralizing the twist energy. If a yarn's twist energy could be neutralized, the yarn would relax because all twist forces vanish if the twist energy vanishes. The finishing process discussed in the following chapter will explain techniques used to neutralize any residual forces, left or right, by neutralizing the twist energy of the fibers.

Active "S"
Twist in skein over-
plied. Active "S" yarn
plies back upon itself
to create a "Z."

Active "Z"
Twist in skein under-
plied. Active "Z" yarn
plies back upon itself
to create an "S."

Relaxed Twist
Skein is balanced.

Relaxed Ply
Twist in singles
now vertical.

Examples of Twist Force in
Plied Yarns

Singles

Singles do not have any balancing force, only the clockwise twist force. Does this means we cannot use singles? No. It does mean that we need to learn how and when to use them. In weaving there are two separate sets of yarns, one vertical and one horizontal, passing over and under each other to create woven fabric. Singles can be use in weaving, as they have been for eons. In fact, highly twisted singles with active twist forces can be used to create interesting textures.

Singles in knitting behave differently. During the revival days of handspinning, many were unaware of the problem active twist can create in knitwear. The result was that singles gained a bad reputation that they do not deserve. Active twist draws the knit structure out of alignment, skewing it left or right, depending on whether the yarn was spun "Z" or "S" as shown in **Twist Force in Singles Yarn**.

The twist force can be neutralized (set) in the finishing process if the twist does not exceed certain levels, depending on the size of the yarn. Whereas the twist force is neutralized in balanced plying, twist energy is neutralized in the finishing process by the application of heat and moisture to the internal structure of the wool. (When the twist energy is neutralized, so too is the force. In balanced plying, the force is neutralized but not the energy.) You can safely spin fine wools into medium weight yarns (14-16 wpi) at a 30 to 39 degree twist angle; medium wools into heavy weight yarns (10-12 wpi) at

"Z" twist singles yarn.

Neutralized "Z" develops furrows as left side of stitch dominates; the more the twist, the deeper the furrow.

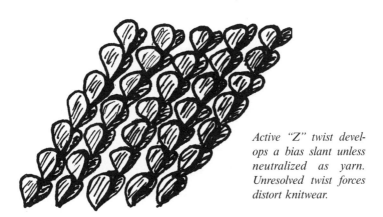

Active "Z" twist develops a bias slant unless neutralized as yarn. Unresolved twist forces distort knitwear.

Twist Force in Singles Yarn

a 21 to 30 degree twist angle; medium and long wools into into bulky yarns (8 or less wpi) at a 14 to 21 degree twist angle as shown in the diagram **Spinning Singles for Knitwear**.)

At higher levels of twist the surface appearance of a knitted fabric develops furrows as shown in **Twist Force in Singles Yarn:** one-half of the knit stitch appears fat and wide (the twist lines are approximately vertical) while the other half of the stitch is skinny, creating a decided vertical ridge. As a general rule, the finer the yarn, the greater the twist level possible. It has also been my experience that the finer the crimp in the fiber, the more readily twist energy can be neutralized, so I use a medium wool with tight crimp for bulky singles even though they have a relatively short staple length. The long wools have good length for a softly spun yarn but the open, wavy crimp, makes a dense yarn with twist more difficult to neutralize.

I particularly like to use singles in both my knitting and tapestry weaving. There is a long history of use of singles in knitting, including the tradition of bulky Cowichan sweaters and the much older traditions preserved in Eastern socks. In the later case, sportweight singles are favored in parts of Turkey, while combining singles without benefit of plying is common practice throughout the region.

Plied Yarns

Singles yarn can be combined to make two, three, four or more strands into the final

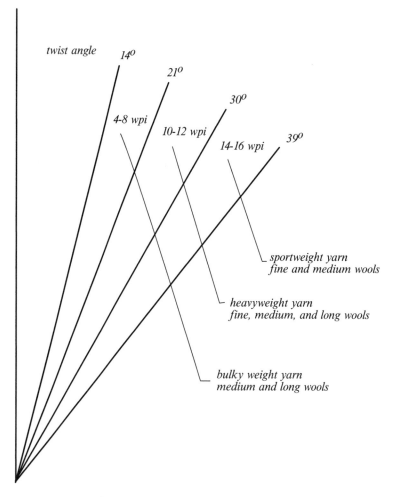

twist angle

14°

21°

30°

39°

4-8 wpi

10-12 wpi

14-16 wpi

sportweight yarn
fine and medium wools

heavyweight yarn
fine, medium, and long wools

bulky weight yarn
medium and long wools

Spinning Singles for Knitwear

yarn. For handspun used in knitting, two and three-ply yarns are probably most common (two-ply in older ethnic pieces). Of the plied yarns, I prefer two ply because it seems to create a more robust, energetic hand and appearance. A three-ply yarn is more softly rounded, with an enhanced propensity to drape—great for cowl necks and shawls. For me, a four-ply is bland and somewhat lifeless (though very durable) while a five-ply is masochistic.

Since singles can be used, why bother with plying? The answer is strength and durability. More twist can be inserted into the singles and twist increases strength, up to a point. With greater twist more fiber ends are contained, so pilling is reduced while resistance to abrasion is greatly enhanced. As a general rule, the more plies, the greater the final strength and durability of the yarn.

If the twist force is neutralized in the plying process, the yarn will be balanced and can be used anywhere. Many spinners will tell you to check a newly plied section: if the yarn hangs in a straight, relaxed loop, it is balanced. But this is not always the case. The twist can be temporarily set while stored on the handspindle so that it does not exert its full force against the ply twist. Such a yarn judged in the manner described will then be underplied. The longer the singles are stored and the higher the temperature and humidity, the more temporary setting will occur. Instead, I always refer to the plied section on the spinning guide described in the last chapter. When a newly spun length of singles is plied back on itself, the resulting two-ply will be balanced. A sample must be made of newly spun yarn to determine balance with three or more plies. The sample yarn must be relaxed, exhibiting no residual twist force.

Cabled Yarns

For cabled yarns, you must spin the singles in one direction, over-ply in the opposite direction, cable to balance in the first direction. Why would you go to this much effort? Possibly you would want to compensate for reduced strength and/or durability in the fiber. For instance, Merino does not make a good sock yarn in its usual state of singles or two-ply. But if you were to spin worsted singles, ply and cable, Merino can make a yarn with incredible softness with sufficient durability for socks. And cabling a two-ply makes a visually lovely yarn.

The How-To of Multi-Plying Strands

Plying on a handspindle is seldom addressed. I have often wondered why, finally coming to the conclusion that most spinners today have not found a comfortable way to ply their handspindle spun yarn. There are a number of traditional ways in ethnic traditions described in the illustrations **Some Less Satisfying Plying Techniques** on the following pages, but I found none that particularly suited my needs.

One of these methods was common in such diverse cultures as Eastern European and Salish Indian. It involves threading the singles from the ground, up through an over-

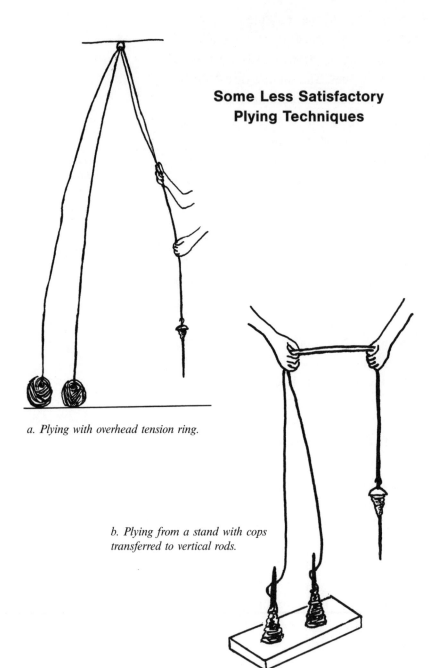

Some Less Satisfactory Plying Techniques

a. Plying with overhead tension ring.

b. Plying from a stand with cops transferred to vertical rods.

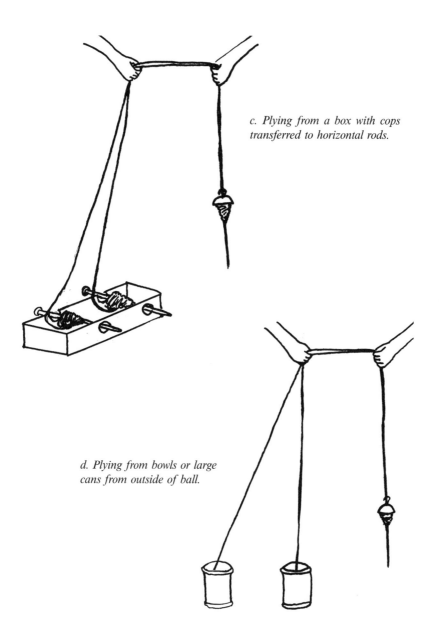

c. Plying from a box with cops transferred to horizontal rods.

d. Plying from bowls or large cans from outside of ball.

Peruvian Hand -Wrap Plying Technique

a. Yarn goes up the back of hand around big finger from right to left, down across beginning yarn and around wrist.

b. Yarn goes up to big finger and around from left to right, then down and around back of wrist.

c. Continue to wrap, alternating steps (a) and (b) until all yarn has been transferred.

d. Yarn on back side of hand.

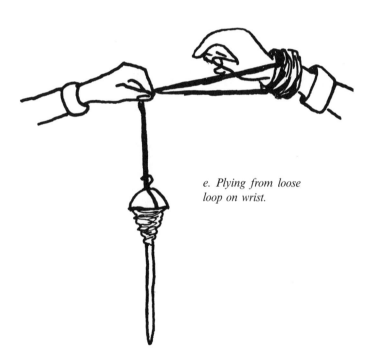

e. Plying from loose loop on wrist.

head ring and attaching them to the spindle. The singles are then under sufficient tension for even plying. But this method does not meet my desire for total portability.

It is also common to ply cops held on a stand or in a box. Without some additional means to tension the yarn, I end up with tangles. I get the same results when the singles are rolled into balls and placed in bowls.

There is a **Peruvian Hand-Wrap Plying Technique** shown on the previous pages which consists of wrapping around the wrist with a crossover on the big finger, unwinding directly from the spindle onto the hand. I find this awkward with all but the smaller spindles so I invert the spindle between my feet, drawing the yarn upward and off the spindle while winding.

The procedure is not complicated. The yarn end should be secured to keep it out of the way just like the roving when spinning the singles. I tuck the yarn under my bracelet, this time on my right arm. Although traditionally the left hand is used, I work off my right and handle the spindle with my left when plying.

To do the wrapping, it is easier to follow the illustrations than the description, but here are the verbal directions: Take the yarn up the back of your hand and around your big finger from right to left. Come down, crossing over the beginning yarn, then around the front of the wrist to the thumb side. Come up the back of the hand again and encircle the big finger from left to right. Come down and around the front of the the wrist on the little finger side. You will have an "X" crossover at the knuckle with angular arms at each side extending to your wrist. At no time does the yarn pass over the palm of your hand, only across the wrist, the big finger, and the back of your hand.

When all the yarn has been wrapped, pull the section at your wrist up (but not off) to loosen the tension. Slide the big finger out of its loop, keeping the loop intact. Push the yarn up to the wrist. Do not tug on the big loop around your wrist or the cross-overs of the finger loop could disengage to open the loop on your wrist. You are now ready to make your two-ply yarn from the two ends. This technique is relatively tangle-free and portable, but it is not my favorite.

When I delved into nomadic techniques of the Middle East and Central Asia I found to my dismay, that in many cases the singles were stored until the people established their living quarters. Then, as a communal activity, the women would gather with a small, crude plying wheel, easily dismantled for packing. Two or three would hold the yarn while another turned the wheel to ply the yarn. A nice idea, but I am a solitary spinner.

Another discovery came about when I was studying the ethnic socks of the region: in many cases, multiple strands were held together without benefit of plying. I am not particularly fond of working with multiple strands because I find it harder to maintain an even tension when knitting.

I still faced the problem of how to ply with total mobility. A popular technique with

Removing Yarn from the High Whorl

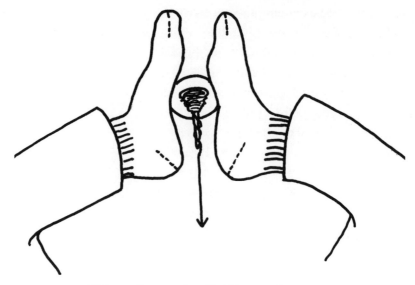

a. With spindle inverted and held between feet, yarn will wind off from around shaft up to nostepinne in hand.

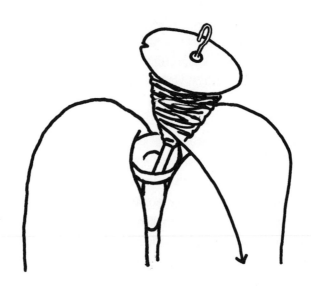

b. With large syringe case braced between knees, shaft of spindle inside is free to rotate while winding onto nostepinne

today's spinners, especially when making samples, is to ply from two ends of a center-pull ball, but I have never been fond of this technique because I always end up with a snarl about two-thirds of the way through. The twist force in the singles is the culprit; when it tried to relax, I was left with a mess no matter how I held the ball.

Then it occurred to me that I wind my knitting yarn into a center pull ball with a nostepinne—why not ply from the nostepinne, keeping it in place throughout the plying process? It worked, taming the snarling induced by active twist. There was an added advantage in that I could push the ball to the wider part of the nostepinne to secure it when I had to discontinue plying temporarily.

Plying off both ends of the ball has advantages beyond that of mobility. Many novice high whorlers tend to spin finer at the beginning, thicker later on when the weight of the spindle has increased. By plying off both ends of the ball, they have a more consistent yarn. And there are no leftovers at the end of plying since one continuous length is being plied.

To ply, the first thing to do is to get the yarn off the spindle and onto the nostepinne (**Removing Yarn from the High Whorl**). I found two simple techniques that work for most spinners. You can turn the spindle upside down, placing it between your feet. I hold it steady by turning my feet on their side with the spindle secured between the arches. By leaning the shaft slightly toward my body,

Winding Yarn onto Nostepinne

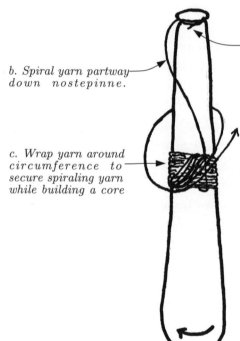

a. Secure yarn by wrapping tip of yarn around notch at top (tip on inside of wrap).

b. Spiral yarn partway down nostepinne.

d. Begin wrapping at forty-five degree angle, rotating nostepinne to advance forty-five degree angle wrap

c. Wrap yarn around circumference to secure spiraling yarn while building a core

the yarn winds off readily. If that method does not appeal, I suggest getting a syringe case (readily available at your local veterinarian in several sizes).

Turn the plastic tube upside down and hold it between your knees. Place the shaft of your spindle into the syringe case. The handspindle will turn freely while you wind off the yarn. The addition of a syringe case does not overload your equipment.

If you have never worked with a nostepinne, how to use it can be a mystery. After all, it is just a tapered stick with a groove cut around the narrower end. This narrow end is the top, the wider portion at the base is where you place your hand for turning. You can use either your right or left hand to hold the nostepinne (**Winding Yarn onto Nostepinne**). With the other hand, wrap the end of the yarn securely around the groove several times. For the yarn to be secured, the end of the yarn must be under the ensuing wraps. When the yarn is secured, take the yarn down the shaft where it is wide. With the hand holding the nostepinne, hold this yarn down with your thumb. Make several wraps around the circumference to secure the yarn in place. Continue to wrap to build a small central core. Then begin to wrap at about a 45 degree angle over this core. After several wraps, turn the nostepinne slightly to advance the wrapping to a new section. Continue in this manner until all the yarn has been transferred to the nostepinne.

You are now ready to make a two-ply yarn. Tie the two ends together with an overhand knot and slip the hook of the spindle through the loop thus formed. Drawing out an even length from both the inside and the outside of the ball, roll the handspindle in the opposite direction from that of spinning the singles. If the yarn does not readily release from the inside of the ball, slip the ball upward to a more narrow portion of the nostepinne.

For singles, I control the spindle with my right hand, rolling up my right thigh. To ply, I reverse the process, holding the handspindle with my left hand, rolling up my left thigh for plying. Plying does not require as much twist as the singles, thus one good roll of the shaft will ply a considerable length. I am lucky to have a balcony off my studio from which I can ply a great length, wind it up around elbow and tip of the nostepinne, then wind on the shaft of the handspindle. (I cannot spin the singles in this manner for I have no means of continuing the rotation of the spindle when the yarn extends below my reach.)

Another means of plying is to use what I have come to refer to as **Plying Sticks**. Actually, they are an old pair of big, wooden knitting needles. For this kind of plying, I use the bright colored leader. After filling the handspindle, I put the point of the needle against the end of the shaft. Holding these together with one hand, I carefully slip the cop into the plying stick. I repeat the process with another cop, slipping it onto a second plying stick. The base of the cop will be at the pointed end with the bright leader highly visible. I put both sticks in my right hand, the

Plying Sticks

a. Cop slipped to wooden knitting needle for plying.

b. Plying from two knitting needles.

points coming out between thumb and first finger, first finger and second finger. The inverted cops are securely held in the cup of my hand. I draw the leaders out and remove them, secure the two ends together with an overhand knot and begin plying as before, this time from the center of the two balls. This is a particularly good method for those who have a plying whorl for increased weight, as the size of the skein can be doubled.

For a three-ply yarn, I spin smaller cops, winding them into three individual center pull balls that I can hold in my hand. With an end coming out between each of my fingers, I am ready to ply as before. Some like to put the balls in separate bowls, spinning from the outside of the ball. I have difficulty maintaining a constant tension on the singles and find that the balls tend to tangle too readily.

A four-ply yarn takes us back to the nostepinne and a plying stick. I slide the cop on the stick as before, drawing out the bright leader to locate the center. I secure the interior and exterior strands together and wind them onto the nostepinne. Then, I ply the double strand from the inside and outside of the ball on the nostepinne (**Plying from Nostepinne**). The end result is a four-ply yarn. If you do not like using the plying stick, you can spin two separate cops, roll them into balls and then wind onto the nostepinne with a strand from each.

The most exquisite multi-ply yarn is achieved with cabling, my preference a 2-ply,

Plying from Nostepinne

4-cable yarn. I spin the singles "Z", then wind it onto my nostepinne. I now ply "S" with excess twist (i.e., over-ply) and again wind onto my nostepinne. The twist is required in plying since the next step involves doubling the plied yarn (repeating the "Z"). The resulting yarn should be balanced.

And now the problem that all spinners face when plying. A strand breaks. There are three remedies. The first is to open up the twist at each side of the break, and splice the yarn into one. This can be time consuming and frustrating because a break usually occurs in a fine, highly twisted section. A second solution, simple to achieve, is overlapping the broken ends by 2–3". Care must be taken to have the broken end securely positioned between the two plying strands. Mill production gives me a third option: knot the two ends together. Lay the ends from the knot in opposite directions. Hold the ends in place while inserting the ply twist. This makes a secure, nearly invisible join.

7

Yarn Finish

To have a finished yarn, the first step is skeining. The oldest skeining method is to wrap the yarn around a body part, such as foot to knee or hand to elbow. This is fine if you have a strong, flexible body. I do not.

I use the simplest tool possible, a stick with two crosspieces: the niddy-noddy. Some consternation can be expected when first faced with a niddy-noddy, for the crosspieces are at 90 degree angles to one another. Positioning the handspindle to wind off, hold the yarn end against the upright in the middle, go up and over the first arm, down and around the second arm, up and over the third, down and around the final arm. A continuous circle is now complete. Continue in this manner until all the yarn has been removed from the spindle.

Let us give cheers for that age when again many beautiful unsigned goods are produced. I look forward to the time when again such beautiful goods are used as a matter of course in daily life.

—Soetsu Yanagi

The beginning tail and the ending tail are tied off together. With waste yarn I then weave four to six ties through the strands, working my way around the circle. This will prevent hopeless tangling in the next step. The yarn is now ready to slip off from an

Skeining

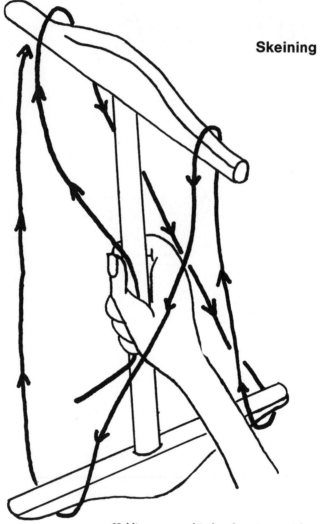

a. Holding yarn end in hand against upright, wind a continuous circle around cross-arms of niddy-noddy.

arm of the niddy-noddy, allowing the skein to fall free (The steps are illustrated in **Skeining**).

I have often heard it said that I "boil my yarn". This is not true. All of my yarn goes through a simmer bath. This step is especially important for singles, as the twist must be neutralized if the end product is to be some form of knitwear. I prepare a warm bath in a large enameled canner (it must be a non-reactive pot—enameled is cheaper than stainless steel). There must be sufficient water to allow the yarn to move freely. Add a little liq-

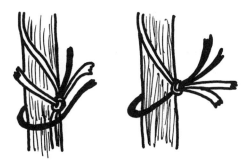

b. Before removing skein from niddy-noddy, tie ends together with contrasting yarn. Loop contrast yarn loosely around all strands of skein, tieing ends together with overhand knot. Contrast yarn will identify beginning. Then loosely weave ties through skein between crossarms. Remove from niddy-noddy.

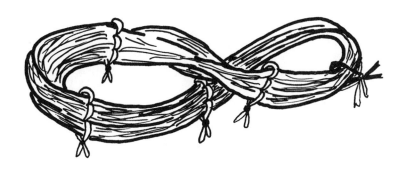

c. Completed skein ready for finishing bath.

uid dish detergent and place the pot on the stove. Add the yarn, set the burner at medium to medium high and slowly raise the temperature to a simmer, not a boil (about 160-180 degrees).

Lift and turn the yarn regularly so all yarn is heated evenly. For woolen yarns, once a simmer is reached, turn the burner off and allow the yarn to cool down until the water is comfortable to the hand. For worsted yarns, once the simmer is reached, reduce the heat to maintain the simmer for about ten minutes, then proceed as with woolen. Why the difference in woolen and worsted? Woolen is open and lofty, easy for the water to penetrate. Worsted is dense, making penetration more difficult. You must make the judgement as to which procedure to follow, that of woolen or worsted for the hybrid yarns—which fall decidedly in neither category.

If the yarn is to be dyed I skip the simmer bath and use the dye bath to fulfill the finishing requirement. Much of my work in the past has been with natural colored wools. My adage: I approach dyeing like death—I stay away from it as long as I can. Today I find myself doing a lot more dyeing because I want the colors of the traditional Eastern socks, especially those of Central Asia. At this point, I use synthetic dyes as I am not particularly knowledgeable about the science of dyeing. To achieve the "old color pallet" I over-dye natural colors. If I want a heathery appearance, colored wool and white wool are blended prior to spinning, over-dyed after spinning.

Straightening the Finished Skein

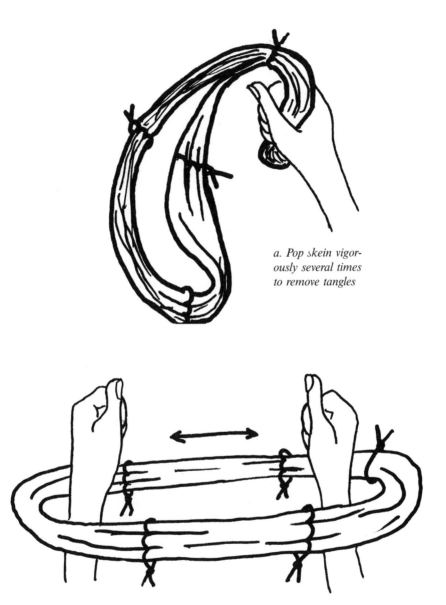

a. Pop skein vigorously several times to remove tangles

b. Snap outward vigorously. Working around skein, repeat several times until skein is tidy and even. Hang to dry—do not block knitting yarns. Some weaving yarns should be weighted to block while drying, especially wrap.

After the simmer bath or dye bath, I thoroughly rinse the skeins in warm water. This may require several rinses to have clear water at the end of the final rinsing. The skeins then go through the spin cycle only on my washer. Upon removal, I grab each skein by the end and pop it like a whip, repeating the popping at the other end (**Straightening the Finished Skein**). Then I place my hands into the middle of the skein, snapping my hands outward to straighten all the yarns. I work my way around the skein, snapping outward several times. Knitting yarns are just hung to dry, not blocked by any means. (Blocking refers to drying the yarn under tension.) Yes, even my singles yarns hang free. Blocking a knitting yarn will reduce its elasticity and loft. The first wetting will relax the yarn and alter the gauge, so that the garment will have to be blocked every time it is washed if it is to fit properly. Weaving yarns can be blocked, especially those destined for the warp.

The yarn is now a finished product. To store the skeins, I grasp them at each end, twist the two sides together firmly, then allow them to ply back on themselves, tucking one end into the loop of the other end. To wind center pull balls for use, I drop the skeins over a chair back and wind the ball on my nostepinne.

Storing the Skein

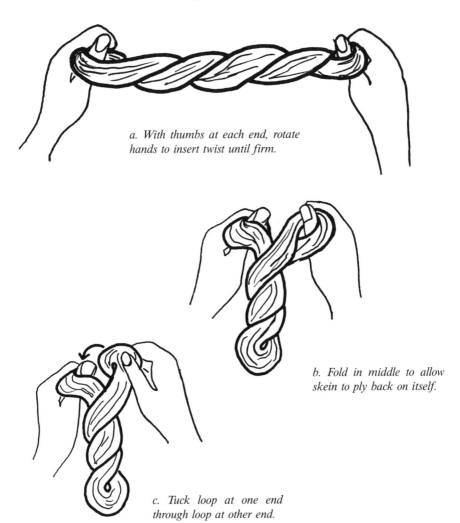

a. *With thumbs at each end, rotate hands to insert twist until firm.*

b. *Fold in middle to allow skein to ply back on itself.*

c. *Tuck loop at one end through loop at other end.*

d. *Skein ready for storage.*

Afterword

I think of myself as a simple person, seeking a less complicated life—not an easy task in today's world. High whorling meets my needs, both physically and psychologically—it is a simple, uncluttered task, earthy in all aspects. Perhaps it is this primitiveness that appeals. From this simple tool I can produce yarns for socks that speak of other times, other places. Or I can weave a tapestry rug, ageless in concept and appeal. Both are primitive art forms that mentally free me from a complex, cluttered civilization. If you are like me, perhaps high whorling will touch your heart and free your soul.

SELECTED SOURCES

Autumn House Farm
RD1 Box 105
Rochester Mills, PA 15771
(412) 286-9596
 Karakul and Karashire fleece, custom blend
rovings.

Carolina Homespun
190 Eastridge Road
Ridgeway, VA 24148
(540) 957-1174
 Basic 75 gm beginner's spindle with friction
fit whorl for both high and low whorl spinning, Mongold spindles, prepared fibers and
custom blends including cotton-wool roving.

Dan L. Mongold
 327 South Bozeman Ave.
 Bozeman, MT 59715
 (406) 586-3794
 Top whorl spindle with semi-circle notches,
swan's neck hook, grooves on shaft, 45 &
70 gm. "Norge" down-shaft whorl spindle in
development.

Ely Sheep Company
12101 South Mulino Road
Canby, OR 97013
(503) 266-4573
 Romney and Columbia fleece, full range of
carded and combed wool.

Iina Ranch
The Navajo Lifeway
P.O. Box 471
Pinon, AZ 86510
(520) 725-3300
  Navajo churro fleece, roving, related Navajo products.

Louise Heits
Icelandic Wools
P.O Box 53
Camden, DE 19934
(800) 777-9655
  Top whorl spindle with high stainless steel hook, drawknife shaft, 10 & 50 gm.

Lynn DeRose Mason
2805 S.E. 34th Avenue
Portland, OR 97202
(503) 236-3127
  Traditional Akha spindles from Southeast Asia

Misty Mountain Farm
10266 Stillhouse Road
Delaplane, VA 20144
(540) 364-1947
  Finn and Finn-Lincoln fleece, prepared fibers.

Norsk Fjord Fibers
P.O. Box 271
Lexington, GA 30648
(706) 743-5120
  Removable top whorl spindle with optional plying whorl, threaded shaft, 75 & 120 gm.

Nordic down-shaft whorl, friction fit to shaft, 25 & 65 gm. Nostepinnes. Imported Spelsau fleece.

The River Farm
Rt 1, Box 471
Fulks Run, VA 22830
(800) USA-WOOL
  Spinner's nostepinne designed with steep angle, no turnings, shallow groove. Mongold spindles. Corriedale fleece, prepared fibers.

Woodchuck Products
114 Woodside Dr.
Clarks Summit, PA 18411
(717) 586-6162
  Double whorl spindle, excellent friction fit of both whorls to shaft, 40 gm top, 60 gm both whorls, related tools.

SUGGESTED READING

Buchanan, Rita. "Mastering Twist," *Spin-Off Magazine*. Vol. 21, #4. Loveland, C0: Interweave Press, 1997

Buchanan, Rita & Robson, Deborah. "Introduction to Spinning" & "Low Tech, High Satisfaction," *Spin-off Magazine* Brochures. Loveland, C0: Interweave Press. 1995

Crowfoot, Grace M., *Methods of Handspinning in Egypt and the Sudan*, Halifax, England: Bankfield Museum Notes, 1931.

Davenport, Elsie G. *Your Handspinning*. Pacific Grove, CA: Select Books, 1964

Hochberg, Bette. *Handspindles*. Santa Cruz, CA: Bette & Bernard Hochberg, 1980

Hochberg, Bette. *Spin, Span, Spun*. Santa Cruz, CA: Bette & Bernard Hochberg, 1979

Gibson-Roberts, Priscilla A. *Ethnic Socks & Stockings*. Sioux Falls, SD: XRX, Inc., 1995

Gibson-Roberts, Priscilla A. *Salish Indian Sweaters*. St. Paul, MN: Dos Tejedoras Fiber Arts Publications, 1990

Gibson-Roberts, Priscilla A. "Summer Spinning, A Return to the Handspindle," part 1, and "Handspun Yarns for Ethnic Socks," part 2. *Knitter's Magazine* #35 & #36. Sioux Falls, SD: XRX, Inc., 1994

Gibson-Roberts, Priscilla A. "The High Whorl Handspindle," *Spin-off Magazine*, Vol. 19, #1. Loveland, C0: Interweave Press, 1995

Mason, Lynn DeRose. "A Spindle Miscellany: Akha Spinning," S*pin-off Magazine*, Vol. 19, #1. Loveland, C0: Interweave Press, 1995

Raven, Lee. *Hands On Spinning.* Loveland, C0: Interweave Press, 1987

Index